THE SPLINTERED HEART

THE SPLINTERED HEART

Conversations with a Church in Crisis

Edited by
Eamonn Conway & Colm Kilcoyne

VERITAS

First published 1998 by
Veritas Publications
7-8 Lower Abbey Street
Dublin 1

ISBN 1 85390 344 2

British Library Cataloguing
in Publication Data.
A catalogue record for
this book is available
from the British Library.

The painting reproduced on p. 129 is *Kitchen Maid with the Supper at
Emmaus* by Velázquez. Reproduced courtesy of the National Gallery of
Ireland.

Cover design by Bill Bolger
Printed in the Republic of Ireland by Betaprint Ltd, Dublin

CONTENTS

Contributors 159

INTRODUCTION

Last year, a week-long conference on the Churches and the media was held in All Hallows College in Dublin. The conference was attended by official Church people and media professionals but it was also open to the general public.

Some of the papers read at the conference were published under the title *Twin Pulpits*. The book was well received. Its success has led to *The Splintered Heart*. This book examines the function in society of the Churches and the artist.

Just as the media and the Churches both trade in 'news', the artist and the Churches are both concerned with the transcendent. Both tell stories and use images to reveal their truths. They push language and symbol into meanings beyond their limits. The priest and the poet minister to mystery. Ideally, they should appreciate and complement each other's craft.

More often than not, they don't. The Churches and the artist are more likely to see each other as rivals. At its most destructive, the rivalry leads to caricature, with the Church saying the artist teaches anarchy and fades boundaries and preaches disrespect for immutable truths, and the artist retorting that the Church dulls the soul and is happy only with the obedient philistine.

At this point in our culture, it is important that the Churches and the artists talk to each other because, just now, that culture is changing shape. The role of the artist is increasing and that of the Church diminishing. New imagery is pushing hard against the old. There is a a danger that we will see it simply as a struggle between old ways of saying things and new ways of imaging them. Those in either camp who have an axe to grind will want a winner and a loser. That would both splinter and starve the heart.

Instead, the real job for both Church and artist is to inherit each other's wisdom and to respect the way they each express it.

That is the value of this book. It brings together people who have committed themselves to either the arts or the Church; in many cases, to both. They write about what art and the Church should be giving each other and where integrity demands they keep their distance.

The Splintered Heart is a celebration of mystery: what the Church calls sacrament, what the artist calls 'the secret threshold'. It is written by people who have long since committed themselves to honest exploration. There is a rich range of attitudes towards the Church and towards art. Some have reached a peace and have decided the place of Church and art in their lives. Others have not and their work reflects their edginess.

It is hoped that this book on the Churches and the artist will be a worthy companion to the previous book on the Churches and the media. We want to thank all the contributors. And we wish to record our appreciation to All Hallows College for encouraging both *Twin Pulpits* and *The Splintered Heart*.

Colm Kilcoyne
Eamonn Conway

WHISTLING IN THE DARK

OR

A JOB FOR JOURNALISTS IN THE TOWER OF BABEL

Colum Kenny

Now the whole earth had one language and few words.

Babble brook. Blabber bedlam. Welcome to the Tower of Babel. You have reached the Information Age. Communicate. Communications. Drown all silence. Be besieged. Throw the off-switch. If you dare.

> *And as men migrated from the east, they found a plain in the land of Shinar and settled there.*[1]

Chatter, chatter, chatter on the talk, talk, talk shows. Hi! Good mornin'! Morning Ireland! Here's the news. Here are the zoos. Plug in. Get hooked. With respect.

> *And they said to one another, 'Come, let us make bricks, and burn them thoroughly'. And they had brick for stone, and bitumen for mortar.*

---

1. This, and the quotations below, are from Genesis 11:1-9.

Do stay tuned. Win a thousand. Win a million. Don't you lose. Be right back. After this break. Enjoy the traumas of our listeners. Easy listening. Easy talking. With our experts by the score.

> *Then they said, 'Come, let us build ourselves a city, and a tower with its top in the heavens, and let us make a name for ourselves, lest we be scattered abroad upon the face of the whole earth'.*

Grab a coffee. Grab a paper. Advance the story. What do they say? Are you ABC or DC? Quality to tabloid, you're targeted. Columnists. Journalists. Bought and sold. Banner headlines. Instant hit.

Climb on board. Start the engine. Catch the Dart. Tune a Walkman. Hear our hi-fi! In-car sound! DAT and DAB. See my CDs. Full system. Make my day. Play my tunes. Build a womb. For the latest. AA Road Watch: 'It's getting worse.'

> *And the Lord came down to see the city and the tower, which the sons of men had built.*

Here I work: on my mobile, on my phone, on line, on coffee, on speed. Information superhighway. Super sad. Background music. Mood muzak. Multimedia. Don't be dull. Time is money.

Here I don't work: Daytime quiz shows. O such fun. Soap and sausage. Agony aunties. Ads remind me what I lack. Uncle Gaybo, am I right?

*And the Lord said, 'Behold, they are one people, and
they have all one language; and this is only the
beginning of what they will do; and nothing that they
propose to do will now be impossible for them. Come,
let us go down, and there confuse their language, that
they may not understand one another's speech'.*

Day is ending. Drive-time up-dates. Catch a movie? Sex and
gore. That's where it's at. Home to TV. Three or four hours.
Everyday. Every night. Watch a video. Pulping fiction.
Pulping fact.

*So the Lord scattered them abroad from there over the
face of all the earth, and they left off building the city.*

Nothing on five hundred channels? There's arcade games.
Compulsive fun to fight machines. Now take a break to walk
the web.

*Therefore its name was called Babel, because there the
Lord confused the language of all the earth; and from
there the Lord scattered them abroad over the face of
all the earth.*

Check the e-mail. Check the voice-mail. Check the teletext,
just in case. Oh my glory! What a wired world! That's the way
they spread their net.

What am I to say? How do I compete? How many million
words will be poured out today on the people? What fortunes
will be expended on convincing them that Coke is the real
thing, that beefburgers make children happy, that Guinness
keeps you fit?

What is left to say when all of the politicians, on all of the chat shows, with all of the 'personalities', have covered all of the angles?

*

I turn on my computer. It gives a nice sharp chime and the screen comes to life. The desktop is bright and businesslike, inviting me to put fingers to keypad. The phrase 'pen to paper' may have a better ring to it but few writers any longer begin their day by actually writing. The modern author should be able to provide copy in a form that can be easily processed. Disks and modems demand no less.

It is not a question of there being nothing on TV. There are dozens of quite good or excellent programmes on television, including some of the American series and comedies which tend to be singled out for scathing comment by European writers. Bashing the Americans, blaming Hollywood for modern forms of communication, may make us feel better but it won't change the fact that Hollywood does it good and people everywhere like it that way.

Piling up words. Who will deny that much of what we tune into is useful, interesting, informative, intelligent? Even more of what we tune into is dross, titillating and sensational nonsense which we as a people lap up. That's the way we like it.

Some writers look at a blank page and cannot bring themselves to write anything. Proverbial writer's block. What happens when you look at the pages of the world and see that they are full, that everything is being said and said again and again and again? That nothing anyone says seems to matter much by next morning?

Whatever you want, you've got it. A magazine on every topic under the sun, and often more than one on the same topic. Expert articles in specialist journals by the score. Dozens of academic publications which exist largely for the vanity of the people who contribute to them and who get career brownie points by listing on their CVs the articles which they have managed to place in them. More and more books of every kind.

Writing is no longer as great a challenge as not writing. To write something, to write anything, is the temptation. If paper never refused ink, our modern communications cacophony never turns down more noise. It is as if we believe that we could build words up to a critical mass from which ultimate meaning might suddenly emerge and save us from ourselves. A tower with its top in the heavens. Tower Records.

In our rush to exchange words we are surmounting language obstacles. Apart from the fact that English is now unofficially but effectively a world language which all are expected to learn and share, various forms of simultaneous and automatic translation ensure that we can get the drift of what the other says no matter what our own tongue is.

We have turned the tables on the Lord of Babel. He coined the motto of the Information Age: 'Nothing that they propose to do will now be impossible for them.' Why, Bill Gates himself could not have put it better!

Rolling breakthroughs in technology have further fuelled the wordsmiths. There are more and more channels available for radio and television services, for video-on-demand, for interactive audio-visual services. Technology allows cheap forms of video production and desk-top publishing. Paper is plentiful.

The worldwide web mocks the writer. Here is a bottomless

pit out of which emerges an endless stream of comment, opinion, fact and fantasy, on every subject under the search-engine. There is no pre-ordained way of distinguishing between what is reliable and unreliable on the net, what is proper and improper. It all presents itself to the web-surfer in an increasingly complex tangle. *There the Lord confused the language of all the Earth.*

Why join in? Why play this game any more? For every word we write there will be a million more written at the same time and put into the public domain. Who is to chose between one and the other?

We can, of course, write to make a living, to make money by providing what is demanded by the market. But write to change the world? Look around and see what the world is reading and tuning into!

A whole public relations and corporate communications sector feeds the frenzy. If it can be written about, well then, pump it out. Have a press release. Have a spokesperson. The system demands it. Don't get left behind. Communicate. Verbally fornicate.

*

And where is religion in any of this? Are there God words? Ought we to count paragraphs, column inches, book titles, minutes of airtime devoted to what is conventionally regarded as religion? To what end? To demand more airtime for priests and nuns, more space for the holy things?

There are indeed God-slots, episcopal press releases, religious affairs correspondents, official spokespersons and the other paraphernalia of corporate religion and its interface with corporate media. There are specialist religious books, magazines and shops. There are diocesan websites. And, in so far as such things have a value, such things have a value. Painting by numbers. Religion by press release and recommended reading.

In the Tower of Babel there is a stairway to heaven marked 'religious section'. It fits in perfectly. Once the right words are in place we will be on our way, on The Way. Institutional communications for an institutional Church.

If Jesus appeared today he would need an agent. He might not be so quick to condemn lawyers as he employed one to close a deal on the world syndication rights of his collected thoughts and sayings. There'd be a movie contract to complete, as well as discussions about the ancillary spin-offs and merchandising. Hey Father! Way to go. Has he a good voice? Not to worry. Our studio boys have ways of making you sing. Build him a Popemobile.

*

There is another way of defining religious writing. This sees it as any writing which tells the truth. This might not always include those press releases which put a spin on the activities of some pope or bishop. But it could include, for example, books, articles and songs by self-styled atheists and agnostics.

The closest some people come to a religious experience in the audio-visual sphere may be a song by the Verve, a film by Fellini or a sensitive documentary about the pain of Aids. Here is Truth. Here is Compassion. Here is the immediacy of Life, in all its vigour and potential. To the people who appreciate this form of spiritual expression, *Songs of Praise* or the broadcasting of a conventional service are dead languages.

In the written arena it is the work of novelists that touches the hearts of this generation, particularly those who bring no claims of grandeur or self-importance to their role in life.

In the context of journalism (it seems to me), religious journalism is that which tells the truth about a matter of relevance to the human spirit. It is a liberating exercise in prophecy, a proclaiming to the world that the truth is accessible and that the truth will set us free. It is not pietistic repetition of archaic formulations of faith or, far less even, the amplification of propagandist press releases or the reassuring massage of bankrupt reformulations of what once passed for faith.

Religious journalism may call forth in the writer a need to criticise religious authorities and vigorously to interrogate received views of the world. At a time such as the present, when it appears that a politically conservative pontiff has conducted a virtual coup within the Church itself, appointing bishops on the basis of their world-view, it is the duty of the journalist who cares about religion to attempt to bring the institutional Church to its senses. This may require the telling of home truths.

It would be wrong to say that the Irish Catholic Church is deeply suspicious, if not hostile, to the media. It would be wrong because the Irish Catholic Church has no representative mechanisms for expressing its views and we cannot say, therefore, what it thinks. The Church is, as Vatican II made us aware, all of the people. It's just that most of the people don't get much of a look in when it comes to articulating what 'the Church' supposedly thinks.

The whole notion of 'the Church' thinking something is quite ridiculous. It is an institution that has no brain. It is made up of people who do have brains and who think very differently about many things, including interpretations of what is appropriate in the religious sphere. Each has her or his conscience and rejoices when, being as true to their conscience as any human being can be, they find a writer who has given voice or body to their own innermost intimations of transcendence, whether through the pages of *Trainspotting* or the more cerebral works of Cardinal Martini or whatever.

In Ireland the 'Catholic Church' is usually taken to mean that very small number of men at the apex of a hierarchical triangle who are bishops. These have no hesitation in speaking out on behalf of the Church in selected areas of life and they have often appeared hostile to any media that is not supine.

They are unhealthily preoccupied with blaming journalists in order to lessen pressure for the reform of the structures that they command. They find it difficult to accept that writers now have more moral authority than they do, which is not to say that writers have much moral authority.

*

For the journalist, attempting to be true to some kind of moral agenda is a formidable task. Unlike bishops, perhaps, journalists are unsure of where precisely the truth lies. They must also exist in a world of editors and audiences or readers. They may be under pressure to pitch their story in a particular way, pressure which can come from the ideology of the owner, be it the state or some press baron or some self-satisfied middle-class trust.

The higher the moral ground, the easier it is for the journalist to feel comfortable. On some obscure programme with a small audience or in some paper where the readership is rich and indulgent it is not too difficult to sound earnest and committed. But it is more difficult to mix it in the world of mass audiences and general readerships and come out of that 'mix' feeling as though one has achieved something worthwhile.

It may be a case of not casting your pearls before swine or it may be more a case of being in the world but not of it. However one looks at the challenge, either one attempts to write in a way that has meaning for society at large or one retreats to a more comfortable perch and talks to the converted. My concept of religion does not preclude controversy, prophecy and sitting down with sinners.

There is scope for a range of religious writing. We must have the utmost respect for a scholar who spends years researching and formulating an academic work which is of interest to only a few but which may ultimately be of value to the world.

We must also acknowledge that in the world as it is we have a need for mouthpieces of conventional wisdom who will articulate in various ways the ideas of the mainstream Church. We should accept that there is a place for such writers and journalists, without regarding them as mere puppets.

But we must also respect the mass media, which can and often does play a constructive role in society, and which has working for it many journalists who see things in less archaic and precious ways than do some who peer through the curtains of bishops' houses. To accept that the religious vocation of the journalist is no less than that of the priest or bishop may seem strange but such acceptance is at the root of a better relationship between the institutional Church and those who write for the media.

None of this is to deny that there are media personnel and

publications whose ethos is hostile to any formulation of serious thinking that might be relevant to the spiritual challenge facing humankind. There are some who are hostile to any religious thought. But short of drawing up a new index of censorship, it is sterile for religious people to engage in public recriminations about particular tabloid titles.

Besides, the recent award of a papal knighthood (what a silly anachronism that institution is!) to Rupert Murdoch has surely given even the most ardent media-basher amongst the Irish bishops food for thought. However, rather than becoming silent they may wish instead to engage in a new form of dialogue with those in the media who still care what the institutional Church says. Contrary to what bishops seem to think, many editors are not obsessed with the Church but find that any coverage, good, bad or indifferent, leaves their readers cold. To that extent the institutional Church has backed itself into a cul-de-sac.

The purpose of a humble dialogue between the bishops and all those who write about religious matters would be to establish mutual respect for all those who are attempting in various ways to articulate a truth that liberates people from their immersion in the world. Such a truth involves acceptance of human limitations all around. Is it not one of the points of the story of the Tower of Babel, that confusion arises when people assume that we can articulate or build a version of reality which is monolithic and absolute?

Wherever there is truth in writing there is religion, and wherever truth is absent then no religious experience is possible. It is not agreement that should necessarily unite us, for that is what by its presumption angered the Lord at Babel. What must unite us is the search for truth, the attempt to find a higher order, a God, in the revelation of his underlying reality. Viewed in this way then even *Pulp Fiction* can be a religious text for some people.

*

There is a tone to some episcopal comment which is likely to infuriate journalists. It comes across as both patronising and paternalistic – not that journalists ought to be surprised. After all, the same tone is deployed to neutralise even priests who do not toe the uncritical line. Words like 'relativist' and 'sensationalist' are part of the vocabulary which goes with the tone. The bottom line seems to be that anyone who disagrees persistently or radically with the orthodox position – a position seldom open for discussion in any forum which does not resemble a fourth year R.E. class – is a misguided person who is at best pitiable and at worst irresponsible and mischievous.

Although well-intended, the contribution of Bishop Thomas *Flynn to Twin Pulpits: Church and Media in Modern Ireland* (Dublin, 1997) is an example of just how far the institutional Church falls short of getting the media onside and how much such contributions still sound as if the speaker is living in the past.

In one of his opening statements Bishop Flynn claims that 'the Church was the first medium with a mission for world-wide communications'. This tells this reader two things. Firstly, the bishop evidently asserts the anteriority and inevitable superiority of Catholicism over all other world-faiths and forms of communications. He dares the reader to disagree with this claim to the ownership of modern communications, although it cannot stand up to serious scrutiny. Secondly, the statement is one of those forced attempts which the institutional Church now makes repeatedly to look as if it is in step with the times. This may impress and reassure the older generation but to many people it seems just as trendy and as phoney as singing priests shows and all of the rest of that awkward regular-guy folksiness.

Bishop Flynn points out in his paper that 'the news media, secular press, radio and television cater for a mass market and they concentrate on what is recent, vivid, entertaining or controversial'. Now the point here is to slight the media while appearing to acknowledge commercial realities. In reality priests every Sunday do what the media does in this respect, getting up on pulpits and finding ways of being relevant while telling the Good News.

Bishop Flynn informs us that 'the media are oriented to the here and now rather than the eternal'. Well pass the collection plate please, Bishop. What is this about? It sounds to me like journalists are being put in their place as mere hewers of wood and drawers of water. The clergy, on the other hand, don't care about the here and now?

'In their need to be vivid and immediate', says Bishop Flynn, 'the modern media simplify; they have very little place for deep reasoning'. Did not Jesus himself reduce the commandments to two and all prayer to the 'Our Father'? Does truth have to be complex? Moreover, there are plenty of reasonably deep articles in our papers and excellent programmes on television. If you want more than that then buy a book. God knows, there is no shortage of them nowadays because book publishing is yet another vast floor of the Tower of Babel. And when it comes to 'deep reasoning', what has the institutional Catholic Church in Ireland done to create places where this can happen?

Bishop Flynn reminds us that 'the media can and do focus

on human failure and abuse within the Church'. By 'Church', of course, he means the clergy and bishops, because 'the Church' employed as a term to indicate the whole people never took off once the Irish bishops returned from Vatican II. Bishop Flynn says of the media covering abuses, in telling words, that 'We cannot object to this'. If he could, would he? Who wants to? Why did the Church not do it itself? Why do the cover-ups continue?

Bishop Flynn is soon demanding that the reader or viewer should know the 'standpoint' of journalists and broadcasters. He explicitly questions the value of 'the all-important concept of balance'. Here is an echo of the Church that for years made people afraid to speak their mind, which has right up to the present hounded even Irish Catholic writers who make bishops uncomfortable, which sacked teachers for not having the right 'ethos'. Thanks, Bishop, but I think that my journalistic concept of balance is a lot more moral than a McCarthyite system of episcopal nods certifying suitability for employment.

The bishop asks, 'What do we mean by balance?'. This curious reformulation of Pilate's famous question, 'What is truth?', is appropriate because there is a real dilemma which journalists face and which they express as the problem of equal time for Judas Iscariot. Should good and bad, as we view them, be balanced? Bishop Flynn puts the question rather more problematically: 'Does it mean, for instance, that when the Pope speaks for the Catholic Church some contradictory voice must be found straightaway to disagree with him in order to achieve balance?' Well, yes, actually, if there is another point of view held by people in our society.

Bishop Flynn seeks the employment of journalists with 'adequate theological formation'. It makes sense that journalists who write about churches and about 'religious' affairs should have some concept of what they are talking about but this again looks like a rebuff to those who write honestly about important religious issues but who do not share the official or orthodox outlook.

Bishop Flynn concludes with an appeal 'to professionals in the media to help make what is important [Church teaching] equally interesting and audience-friendly'. This seems to be a plea for public relations rather than for journalism. If this suggests that his version of reality should take precedence over the truth as I perceive it then I, as one professional, reject his plea.

I will, however, endorse his appeal 'for the return of that good old virtue of forgiveness'. I would love to see the bishops seek forgiveness for the pain which they have caused (not 'may have caused' which is the formulation they prefer) by their actual arrogance and intolerance, by their closed view of the world. Let them not put their trust in spokespersons and media-handling by professionals but in faith. Let them consider the possibility that they presumed to build their own 'tower with its top in the heavens' to make a name for themselves and that the Lord now wants them scattered abroad upon the face of the whole earth.

Let them have confidence in and respect for clergy and lay people who are searching for a Truth which is not easily boxed and let them seek new structures for a message which was never meant to be set in stone. In the meantime, I will ask their forgiveness for any arrogance or any lack of charity on the part of those of us who believe that if we tell the Truth we may shame the Devil and who live in some faint hope that mere words can still induce meaning within the hearts of the people of the Tower of Babel.

THE ANNALS OF HANNAH

Aidan Mathews

Creative writers and Christian ministers are divided by a common love of books. Let me therefore begin to think about texts and contexts, scripture and writing, the Word and the wordprocessor, by quoting from the people of the book at the outset of 1 Samuel in the writings of the Hebrew Bible, that faith-and-culture cornerstone which all Judaeo-Christians, priests and artists, prophets and apostles, persist in calling the Old Testament.

Hannah rose and presented herself before the Lord. Now Eli the priest was sitting on the seat beside the doorpost of the temple of the Lord. She was deeply distressed and prayed to the Lord, and wept bitterly. She made this vow: 'O Lord of hosts, if only you will look on the misery of your servant, and remember me, and not forget your servant, but will give to your servant a male child, then I will set him before you as a nazirite until the day of his death. He shall drink neither wine nor intoxicants, and no razor shall touch his head'.

As she continued praying before the Lord, Eli observed her mouth. Hannah was praying silently; only her lips moved, but her voice was not heard; therefore Eli thought she was drunk. So Eli said to her, 'How long will you make a drunken spectacle of yourself? Put away your wine.' But Hannah answered, 'No, my Lord, I am a woman deeply troubled; I have drunk neither wine nor strong drink, but I have been pouring out my soul before the Lord. Do not regard your servant as a worthless woman, for I have been speaking out of my great anxiety and vexation all this time.' Then Eli answered, 'Go in peace; the God of Israel grant the petition you have made to him.' And she said, 'Let your servant find favour in your sight'.

Eli of Shiloh is a priest, the genteel sentinel of the sacred of the sacred. He guards the approaches *ex cathedra*. Ways in and out, exits and entrances, the thresholds and doorsaddles of the interim realm between pure and profane, earthen and unearthly, are his to invigilate. For he isn't only the janitor of scripture and sacrament: he is the president of transcendence – in other words, an institutional churchman, whether a curial magnate or a minor parish curate. To be sure, this missioned officer can decay into an admissions official, his order into orderliness and his ministry into administration. Then the tent-flap of the pavilion hardens into a portcullis and the authoritative proclamation of the love of God becomes the powerful proclamation of those whose love is unauthorised and therefore godless. But for the moment he merely behaves as if he were the owner-occupier of the holy of holies instead of a bright darn in one little windsock of the Spirit.

Now the Most High God is far above Hannah's head. Because of her menstrual blood and her unchewed breasts, she has learned how pagan and how piggish is the segregation of self and flesh, of heaven and earth, in the bilingual shrine at Shiloh. Her gut feelings are good enough for God's house. Clearly infertile and therefore culturally forfeit, her gender a calamity, her barrenness a catastrophe, she exists in a dry stasis between menarche and menopause, in the irony of her periods and the ridicule of rival concubines. Her own deliverance from the world can only occur as the gift of another's delivery into it. And this is the lamenting and demented paradox whose doxology so disturbs Eli: not, be it said, because she's there at prayer but because her praying and her praise are the template of a different oratory.

'Eli observed her mouth.' What he sees there in the red zero of orality is a labouring birth, the unspeakable struggling toward outspokenness, the teeth and tongue of the woman fashioning a language that is two-thirds plea and one-third pleasure of utterance in a last and lasting cry: 'Open my mouth, O Lord, and my lips will proclaim your praise!' Yet Eli hears nothing (always a trope of stupor in the Hebrew scriptures) because Hannah's petition is not the permitted sort, neither the pilgrim silence of the mute retreatant nor the pious ejaculations of the licensed liturgical drudge. Instead she prays in silence: hers is a strange, subjective deed, personal yet performative. Little wonder Eli rushes in. For this worshipper – no worthless woman, no drunken spectacle, but a true servant of God – is, beyond all sinners and secularists, his real adversary. She is not reading to Yahweh from the closed fonts of a missal; she is speaking to him in a freshwater vernacular.

And the rest is history – the history, at least, of the last century or so in this country. To one side, there's the scandalised insomniacal prelate with his fear of social change and sensual restiveness, his monopoly in the market-economy of local idols, and his right-wing night-terror that the Beatitudes will be the death of the Decalogue; on the other, the artist and writer, Jacobin in his politics, Jacobite in his psychology, articulating at times the exhilaration of God's aboutness, and, at the other moments, confessing great anxiety and vexation, the mystic of kisses for whom the flesh and blood of human beings is the meat and drink of Creation, that rowdy, uncowed incarnational story which God himself is dying to hear.

Now I don't intend to continue trooping these binary pairs. Things are never black and white, not even in amateur chess. Besides, all of us have our token and true anecdotes from the pre-conciliar era, our favourite yarn from the war. Those of them that are sweet are often sweet nothings, the chatty tactic of a premature amnesty; and those that are galling are sometimes sour grapes, too acidic for any carafe of tapwater at the lectern. But a bittersweet in-between fable may serve some purpose. If I choose from the days of sideburns and Biafra to remember a parish priest with stole and sprinkler blessing a new Mercedes in the gravel sweep of our drive, while our Protestant neighbour's sun-hat bobbed at the privet and an orphanage nanny swept past the granite gatepost with somebody else's children plucking at her gaberdine, it isn't only because the image configures capital and creed, but because I was a passenger in the same make and model thirty years later when an elderly Kerryman at the wheel pointed to a psychiatric hospital on a hillside and said to me: 'That is where they locked up homosexuals and women at the change.' And his 'they' signalled, in all the clarity of shorthand, the chaplains, lay and religious, of a confessional and carceral state. His blinking back tears was another matter. The brightness that day would have blinded you.

To tell that tale is also of course to be a tell-tale, for a story about violence cannot omit the violence and violation implicit in all storytelling. In this instance, I've cast myself as the introspective bystander, a casualty and not an accomplice to cultural atrocity. So a whitewash accompanies a blacklist, as it always must. Yet the anecdote reminds us that in our lifetime the Church of the establishment had the time of its life: it was Constantinian but it was never Constantinople; it was Byzantine but it was never Byzantium. The Tsar of Russia declared for the Orthodox instead of the Catholic liturgy because his emissaries reported that the mental elegance of Latin tenets could not compare with the heart-breaking beauty of the Eastern choir; but where was our legendary Torah Talmud, our theological aplomb, when we represented the mystery of Christ incarnate as the mystification of Christianity Incorporated?

Accordingly our hearts rise at the fall of the firm. We do not want it back or forward. The Holy Spirit has flown the coop of Santa Sophia and is nesting, as she should be, in bedsits and at bus-stops. We grieve for the gospel witnesses – often anticlerical, rarely irreligious, never secular – who troubled the Church authorities much in the manner that Jesus of Nazareth did, and whose martyric efforts were rewarded for decades by sanction and scrutiny, by curfew and censorship, by clandestine sabotage and hateful defamation; and we are glad that it was always the demonised and bedevilled writers who recognised the Christ-like, just as it was always the demonised and the bedevilled in Palestine who recognised and acknowledged the Son of Man as the Son of God.

In a way that is both God's Word and the word-of-mouth of men and women everywhere today, we have learned that power is the opposite of authority and that the dismantlement of the one will not immediately robe us in the other. Our congregations dwindle into audiences because some have not been reminded often enough that they are whole and holy, the adored of God; and because others have been reminded once too often that Christ is neither a Roman Catholic nor the puppet of a bourgeois Christendom; and because yesterday's honour guard is always today's gauntlet, a social phenomenon which is not limited to the domain of Om and Amen and which consists in swapping flails and fetishes, Lambs of God and black sheep, in order to scapegoat somebody other than ourselves in the whodunit stakes of our shame-and-blame civilisation.

Lent or Advent, therefore, is a time of preparation, of humiliation amounting to humility, of a lowliness so abased it may be burial, tears turning to sperm, seed in a dark place, the will of the father being done in earth and not above it. And the *post mortem* on the old Jerusalem should be part of the *curriculum vitae* of the new Jerusalem, for neither looks very much like Nazareth, which is a better model for our eventual human encampment than any city-state makeshift.

When I was small, the ecclesiastical bosses blared from their ghastly bullypulpits. Christ in this country spoke the language of Caesar; now, increasingly, it is Caesar who speaks in the language of Christ. Lewis Carroll may be as helpful here as C. S. Lewis, for it is hard to zero in on such full circles. The prince bishops have been truly and truthfully routed by the puritan divines, and a new mood of authoritarian liberalism – which may be a modality of the old culture of control – fumigates the state like the incense of a Corpus Christi procession in the days and decades before the Feast of Bloomsday substituted itself for that forgotten anthropology of bread and circuits. It could be the case, of course, that the reciprocal enmity of scholastic and humanist, of cleric and intellectual, may result only in the ludicrous doubleness of opponents who imagine themselves to be poles apart and whose trenchant dislike masks authentic likeness, as in the Yiddish seanfhocal:

> *When chimney-sweep and baker fight,*
> *Baker turns black and sweep turns white.*

A taste for cleaning the temple can, after all, mature into an appetite for the bullwhip and bullhorn; if this be so, secular homelists could well carve mentors out of their tormentors, since the vitriol of the priestly militia in the past provides impressive copy for today's proconsular sorts. When, in the unimaginable future, victims turn into plaintiffs and plaintiffs into prosecutors; when the discalced columnist graduates into a pillar of the state who laminates his samizdat for the colour supplements, and when the counter-culture itself becomes a tolerated opposition, its perturbation downsized to a *frisson*, its danger miniaturised into decor, this will only be a scale facsimile of the route – no Way! – that led the priest of the Penal era from a chance existence through a lively chancery to the age of episcopal investment portfolios. For the New World sooner or later much resembles the same old world it ousted.

So when I sit in my car in traffic and watch the Christ before me and the Christ behind me and the Christ to my left and the Christ to my right – in short, the persons who are the real presence of God in the world – listen like myself to the same radio bulletins and read like myself from the same newspaper, I encounter and engage already another Karaoke world, the entirety of Ireland turning into County Dublin, as totalised in its own way in my middle age as the theocratic gendarmerie of the 1950s could make it in my childhood. This is neither bad, mad, nor sad; indeed, it could, would, and should be the happy subjunctive of rejuvenation. All it suggests is that perhaps Holy Roman Empires do not require to be either holy or Roman to be at least imperious and potentially imperial, and that the next or nearest Emperor's lack of a wardrobe is immaterial beside the fact of naked power which will always clothe him in the slipstream of excellent sex.

If the new post-Christian culture preserves some aspects of its discredited predecessor, the writers and artists exemplify a lovelier continuity within that unsuspecting mimicry. In the Dublin of my adolescence, there were draughty seminaries with rat-killer in the corridors where it was possible to hear Hausa, pidgin, Yoruba, Swahili, from the mouths of missionaries whose sectarian beliefs had been converted into Christian faith by the barefoot charities of their semi-desert stations, their shanty habitats in the breeze-block South world. Indeed the BBC itself looked upon the Irish religious dispersion as a more comprehensive news service than Reuters because our sisters and brothers were everywhere with their armour-proof copperplate airmail letters. Now, in a new Pentecostal pathfind, the Celts leave Ireland less as Columba the monk than as Colmcille the poet, their exile a commute, their currach a boarding-card, and their white exile a tour of the faculty ghetto, the Creative Writing department and the upstate artists' dacha; but their mission aspirations, the great Go and Tell, remain the gospel truths of ordinary experience as the ground of celebration and commitment. Whether as rock-stars or satirists or cinematographers, poets, playwrights or prose-writers, there is today a sodality of fabulists who oppose the planned, the programmatic, the positivistic, the managerial Anglo-American gluttonies of the late Enlightenment, and the very phallic ideology – via the

Greek twist in our cortex – that the self precedes the Other instead of proceeding from it.

This may not make them practising Roman Catholics or believing Christians – or even practised and believed ones like many of us – but it does make them stewards at the wedding feast in the canvas diocese of Jesus.

That's to say, the artist continues the Acts of the Apostles and is himself, in common with the Deuteronomic authors and the Christian evangelists, an apostolic subject. He is, in terms of our own traditions of reference, Christian. He is not yet Christ, though he discovers himself in the stamina of contradiction and fights for his life in a sum of complexities that would enthral a dialectician. For, as nooses turn into haloes and hedge-schools into summer schools, this ambassador in chains finds that his manacles have alchemised from handcuffs to cufflinks into insignia of immense prestige. Herod's bookshelves creak with our sought and signed indictments of him. Pontius leads the first-night encores at a bitter polemic against the Justice system. Caiaphas and a current Antichrist sink their differences in the warm glow of flashcubes and red wine at a launch. For the state has become so vast it can defend itself against any invasion, like Russia facing Napoleon, by retreating into its own amnesia and awaiting the winter.

As the cultic act of one Church fades from view, the activity of its sacerdotal replica looms larger. Theological institutes close and artists' colonies open. Diocesan lecturers disappear from the varsity concourse and their place is taken by mendicant troubadours as Bohemia puts Moravia in its place. An ABC of Arts Council endowments (from which I have benefited on several occasions morally and materially) begins in air-tickets, bursaries and conference papers, and ends, please God, in the serene status of a Zen master. To the university campusinos who are the chief constituency of the writer, this lifestyle – part walkabout, part withdrawal – is the peripatetic repeat of the medieval practice of itinerant teaching and preaching, and the periodic appearance of paperback fictions offers the aesthetic equivalent of sacramental nourishment. There are works of glittering seniority for which, like the Spiritual Exercises of Ignatius Loyola, only the most diligent of *illuminati* are eligible; there is an intermediate stratum of accessible yet arthoused products and periodicals which are the holy communion of sensible Sunday sorts; and, as one moves from writers to authors, from those who reveal the world to those who reflect it, there are popular works of devotion – newsagent novels, topical and thought-provoking verse, dramatisations of broadsheet broadsides – that enable occasional churchgoers to re-experience the consolatory distraction of Kitsch without traipsing through the transepts.

On the practitioners themselves, from deacons to abbots and Vatican fat-cats, this culture of culture can bestow the lugubrious ambiguities of a professional middle-class *modus vivendi* from which to champion all those unwashed and unbaptised who do not always read books or even want to, the proletarians on the periphery, the pure of heart and the poor in spirit, and from which to critique the ethical deficit of the same continental middle-class polity which is both the market-place and the moratorium of all such protest, as London publishers lubricate our post-colonial prospects and retrospects and the international compare-and-contrast league-tables go on grooming the most gifted scripts of the Zeitgeist until a consensus has condensed into a canon.

Some of these ironies are lenient and inevitable. (They are

the ones that apply to me.) Some are lethal and inexorable. (They are the ones that don't.) Awareness and wariness befit the artist. Any dictionary worth its salt will show you prophecy sweating it out between a rock and a hard place, between profit and prophylaxis. So the innocence of the dove must incubate the cunning of the serpent. Yet from this comedy of socio-cultural abundance, this competitive mix of ashram and shopping arcade, of tightrope and catwalk, Holy Day and bank holiday, the higgledy-piggledy biographical vitality of so much pen and paper, so much origami and carbon, spring-lists and autumn programmes, amazing grace increases and multiplies: in the meticulous equity of Jennifer Johnston's fiction, in the oriental reverence of Michael Longley's poetry, in the tart Chaucerian tenderness of Roddy Doyle's realism, in the Dutch interiority of Sebastian Barry's domestic playscripts, in the profound, redemptive dramas of Neil Jordan's films and the fastidious anguish of John Banville's universe, in the ebony lightness of Paul Muldoon's lyrics and in the Galilean dailiness of Eavan Boland's space-walk through the hall, stairs and landing of our deep indoors; in this, in that, in the other: in Otherness itself.

Pickings from the platter. I could go on, sounding and resounding like a prudential blurb on a book cover; but the point is plain: there are laureates galore in a country no bigger than Birmingham. And they are writing some of the best English of the late twentieth century.

What are they writing about, these artists and writers? They are telling stories. They are telling passionate stories. They are telling passionate narratives. They are telling the story of the passion narrative itself: a story of the liminal and the eliminated, of the outcast and the downcast. And though I believe it is true that the Gospel accounts of the crucifixion of Jesus, more so than any other parallel narratives from late antiquity, gestate the form of the novel as we know it in the West, there's no clear reason why our writers should choose to affirm the Jewish morphology of the story instead of the Greek paradigm, for Athens is the half of our inheritance and the Stoa of Attalos has always intersected with the Porch of Solomon in our cultural atlas, just as Plato's Symposium has always occurred within earshot of the Last Supper. But it's the prophetic and not the Periclean perspective that commands the Irish imagination: and the still surviving urchins of the Eastern Mediterranean, whose oldest oral tradition is the eucharistic sacrifice, stories told over food, continue to prefer the scribbles of the victim to the victor's literature.

The foundational legends of the Greeks are a grim theological summa. I don't so much mean the individual texts by Sophocles and Euripides which constitute, in Simone Weil's expression, a 'fifth gospel', Antigone's dogged agenda. I am thinking rather of the *Iliad* and the complementary chronicles of the House of Atreus, two shared and symmetrical versions of fractiousness and fratricide, of cultural and civilisational ruin, and of their beautiful, ululating anthems to doom and damnation, to exponential manslaughter, which the wise and searing pessimism of the Greeks gave rise to. The Palestinian plot is a different matter. Its tale of trial and retrieval, of suffering and recuperation, windstorms, windfalls, the anointments of pain, God's unexpectedness as the green and menaced venue of our tenting, wrests a destiny out of a fate and derives a new and better mythology – the final privilege of victimhood – from the debris of the victimiser's propaganda.

From the time that Saul of Tarsus crossed from Asia into Europe at the site of the sacked citadel of Troy, that choice between Greek and Judaic modes of storytelling has been as strict as edicts. Even then, it was an ancient rivalry. When the people of exodus and exile bound themselves in their restorationist euphoria to be a people of the book, the posterity of Torah, Thucydides was interpreting in his Peloponnesian history the metallic, retaliatory arithmetic of the war between Athens and Sparta, its cyclone of homicide, a dreary, dreadful tautology of one massacre after another. And so it goes on, the clash between the news and the good news, between communiqués and communication, between the world according to Alexander the Great and the Gospel according to Jesus of Nazareth. In our own time, the conflict took the form and deformation of face-saving superpower pugilism over Cuba, that implacable psychopathology of obsessional rivals locked in the lovers' embrace of a mutual stranglehold, while the first general session of the reforming and transformative Second Vatican Council began, at last, to set aside its age-old megalomania and voodoo in the interests of the dear Master and the many shaloms of Emmanuel.

Much *spes* and some *gaudium* later, the alternative remain: a Greek prospect of hubris from uterus to hearse in the dementia of resentment, or in the Semitic vision, the liberations of apparent failure amid the deliberations of transparent ordinariness.

It is the Palestinian plotline which, for better and worse, our writers thicken. To hear what they are saying we must watch closely like Eli; we must practise listening, the listening of the Lucan Jesus on the road to Emmaus who first invites the bewildered and grief-stricken disciples – like Hannah they are 'deeply distressed' and 'weeping bitterly' – to tell their story fully and fulfillingly, to tender it, to render it, to be rent by it.

He knows what he is doing, this same storyteller, this itinerant minstrel from Galilee, the man whose own fables and fictions always begin with 'Once upon a time', the introit of the curious, discoursing universe, and never start with 'In the beginning', the stately mantra of the contemplative. He is, after all, the sudden, fluent spellbinder whose vivid edition of a woman's existence stills and bestirs her simultaneously so that she calls out, 'Come hear a man who has told me everything about my life!' – surely the very definition of the magnanimity imagination generates. And he is, in talkative addition, the rabbi of ballads, of lullabies, of thumbnail revelations, tragical riddles, prophetic mnemonics, pastoral letters, romantic comedies, scriptural satires, adages, aphorisms, the annals of every Hannah, and all within the middle ground and the medium wave of plain speaking, of the agile, glandular language that lies between the banalities of small talk and the blandishments of encyclicals. So he sits in the fo'c'sle of the fishing boat, with the lake-water's blinding surface an impromptu acoustic aid for the huddled crowds on shore, and he enchants them; or a few of them hunch cross-legged under a handy spruce as it spreads the shade like a tablecloth under its branches, and he enchants them again. He knows what every writer and artist knows: that storytelling is not extraneous and recreational; it is intrinsic and creative. It is as basic as sex and breakfast.

But how could Jesus have been otherwise than wise and other? Isn't the slipshod, god-given, dogsbody plenitude of the Hebrew scriptures themselves a model of narrative proliferation? Chronicles, lyrics, lamentations, myths, memoirs, prayers, politics, philosophy and the Lord knows what, assemble with ecumenical inclusiveness a literature that venerates every human discourse, no matter how bungled or rambunctious, be it scatology or eschatology, as the wetted vowels of Yahweh.

Likewise the Gospels. The good news is all the better for being found in four places at four different times and not in one at the same time. To that extent, the Christian story is anarchic rather than Koranic; plural and therefore playful; affirming the diversity and distinctiveness beloved of the Absolute who invented so many particulars, instead of asserting the grey and unitary hygiene bespoken by apparatchiks. The copiousness of the New Testament reflects something of the manysidedness of Torah and the prophets, and something therefore of the miraculous versatility of the readings that shaped Jesus in a culture of universal literacy. For it is the grace of imagination, embodied in the plasma of living texts, that returns us to ourselves by restoring us to our otherness as guests of our past and ghosts of our future, making us strangers to ourselves at first in order to make us stranger than ourselves at last. And if we wish to secure the hazard of such grace we must read all our stories, sacred and secular, the immortal and the eternal, not as the plenipotentiaries of a lectionary but as part of the whole planet at matins.

And we must do more than that to do at least that much.

We must re-imagine our sacraments as well as our scriptures, for christenings and weddings and funerals have become the new missionary horizon of the urban millennium, a 'Come and see!', not a 'Look here, you!', a line drawn in the sky and not in the sand and so an arc instead of a limit. For the community of believers is only a part of the whole and wholesome people of God. Beyond the Christian and the post-Christian and the non-Christian there is the paschal mystery of a human universe in the chrysalis of its own pain and aspiration, a radius beyond any diameter. Recalling this, we must breathe life into the dead weight of our liturgies by inhaling their forgotten fragrances, their hidden beginnings. Wildflowers quiver in the pot-pourri, cloudbursts weep in the bandaged tap, pollen sinks in the house-dust; and the primal appeal of our rites of incarnation – font and paten, ash and chrism – has been dehydrated to the point where plastic chips from plane geometry can still be called upon to signify celebratory companionship in the name of the Crucified and where many of the lesser customary practices of the Western patriarchate are only written in stone because they are fossil fragments.

We must re-imagine baptism. The knowledge of water is not H_2O; it is thirst. The knowledge of baptism is the experience of our dependence on the freshness and refreshment of the other. It is physical – and therefore metaphysical too – but it is not abstract or abstruse. It is our life between the well and the waterfall, between the secret source and the manifest abundance. It is the skeletal garden greening in all its jewellery because the Covenant stands and because life is possible only in the translucent moment between the deadness of steam and the deadness of ice. It is the elation of the parched throat and the bloated tongue, the echoing canticle of the coolness sliding inside us. And it is saltwater too, the harder hospitality of the deep. For the saline smell of our own genitals brings us the odour of our origins, our stranded marine identity, gills and tail-fluke of the embryo, our total immersion as a boat people. So the separation of water from water in the myth of the second day, the cramped jeopardy of the Ark, the night-crossing of the Red Sea, the brackish shallows of the Jordan and the tiny, tumultuous thread of silver that Jesus stepped across when he waded into the Kedron, are all tropes of endurance and duration in an element – God's love – which is life-giving yet lethal, like the drowsy sac of salty water in which the foetus curls into a question mark before the flood buoys her along the birth canal.

We must re-imagine penance. The virtual extinction of the traditional form of sacramental reconciliation in our time reminds us that such re-imagining must be ongoing, for auricular privacy in the Counter-Reformation was itself a bold break with the public profession of guilt in an earlier period, and is usefully preserved even today in the structured silences and intimacies of modern clinical counselling. If the confessional is doubling as a storage space for the vacuum cleaner these days, it isn't because contemporary Catholic Christians are libertarian boors but because the occasion is spiritually inadequate to the stature of their yearnings for the Lord's good encouragement and endearments. That yearning finds expression in a thousand unburdenings, from session therapy to the ministerial presence of loved ones, and if, as we believe, God assumes flesh in the kindness of human hands, then these are sacramental and sanctifying encounters in which we do experience the terrible textual intricacy of our lives both as analysis and as *analusis* – the look-alike confusion of our corner-stones and stumbling-blocks; the identity of our strengths and weaknesses; the alibis of our egotism, the aliases of our jealousies; the recognition that we can be rescued by a vice and defiled by a virtue; the urge, above all else, to find someone to blame – and then emerge magnified in the force-field of our wheat and tares, the sum of our humble harvest festival.

We must re-imagine eucharist. Alb and altarcloth can so bedazzle us that we fail to bless the eucharistic loveliness of a shared take-away in a digs or the grace of the separated Saturday dads queuing with their kids for a styrofoam banquet in McDonald's. Wherever food becomes a meal in the moment of timid community, there is eucharist; wherever bread is broken together or the chalice drained in a solitariness that strives for mutuality, there is eucharist. And the real presence of Christ in loaf and cup should not deflect us from the real presence of Christ in the priest who breaks and blesses, in the grubby toddler who has defecated into her diaper during the Prayer of the Faithful, in the teenage biker with her nipple ring whose foot has gone to sleep up in the gallery during the Communion reflection, in the emphysemic newspaper-seller in the porch whose tongue is crusted with lemon from the endless antacid tablets as the recessional hymn starts, or in the oriental grandmother at the zebra crossing whose handbag matches her shoes and who is rummaging in the lining of her anorak for the small change that has slipped through a hole in her pocket because she has given all the pound coins she had to the first and second collection.

It is these and no other that are the acceptable sacrifice. These are the children God is feeding with his own flesh and blood as a mother feeds her foetus with the rich red bloodstream of her body.

We must re-imagine marriage, its passion and compassion, eros and labour, the apostolic succession of one wrestling, head-first body bulging out of another, of one woundedness pressing a smaller vulnerability into the embedding world. After all, it is to a wedding feast that Jesus of Nazareth calls us, not to a church service. The antibiotic solemnities of the nuptial liturgy rather recoil from the incarnational radiance of men and women as God delights in them: in our dailiness, in our dinginess, in the storm-damage of our bed-linen and the *mappa mundi* of the stains on our sheets. Yet sacramental culture surely exists to manifest the pre-existing sacredness of the world that God has ordered for freedom, and that sacredness is not sufficiently celebrated by a tradition of faith in which the balance between Catholicism and catholicity is more often academic than actual.

How many persons leave a church after a wedding in the realisation that they continue the Creation, as the spouses of the cosmos and partners of the Spirit, through raising a family on limited funds in, say, 1001 The Fairways, Woodbrook Glen; that they are really and truly eternity's only calendar, and that they are the incarnational momentum of God's dream as the Word assumes flesh in a universe which is more eucharistic with every sharing of self and sparing of other? How many leave in the sudden, dumbfounding gladness that their relationships, whether regular or regulated according to the small print of the bigwigs in birettas, are uncontrollably revelatory of the Lord's exhilaration in his darlings? How many go in the knowledge that their secret Nazareths, to the oblivion of all tabloids, are the spirit's safe houses and not the public basilicas of a jurisprudential Jerusalem where, always, God is exalted and Jesus is crucified?

Yet these are the persons who are bringing Christ into the world, not through the abracadabra of magic but out of the humdrum bric-à-brac of their own curriculums, a job, a hobby, an obsession, just as the Celtic manuscript illuminators fleshed out Jesus in the pigments of beetroot, nettle, and the egg-yolk of a puffin.

Finally we must re-imagine suffering and death, not as fundamental but as foundational, the haunt of flesh and blood, as basic to being as carbon to chemistry. We cannot avoid them by restoring personalist devotional practices under the sign of the soul or by persevering in the collectivised anguish of social praxis under the sign of community. Neither the work of the Lord nor the Lord of the Work will ever turn the Cross into a tree or a roof-tree. Not even aesthetics will anaesthetise it. So our requiems must rediscover their restlessness. From self-serving motives of phoney consolation, we must not talk the language of Easter Sunday so blandly in the presence of Good Friday. Instead, we must make room in our order of worship for silence and rage, as much for barbarous, infuriated hurt as for clubbed and brutalised hope. At the end of the day, it is not James and John who flank Christ on the cross; rather, as darkness falls, it is the two terrified and enraged thieves, the godless and the guilt-ridden, who despair and die there. Only by assenting to the undiminished immensity of loss and leave-taking can our hearts become, eventually, as empty as the tomb on Easter morning and as broken as the women whose story of that same emptiness was dismissed by the inconsolable apostles, fresh from a blue-bottled corpse, as an old wives' tale. For the language of cross and resurrection, of the two raising-ups, remains a homiletic hoax unless it asserts as well the terrible temporal incoherence of the burial in between.

The first European to be baptised was, famously, Lydia of Philippi, the handmaid of the Macedonian mission. But Paul did not discover her in this or that ecclesiastical alcove. She was not the catechumen of any other Christian Jewish missioner nor the proselyte of a Hellenised synagogue. More simply, on the sabbath, as Luke tells us in the Acts, the Jews for Jesus 'went outside the gate by the river, where we supposed there was a place of prayer; and we sat down and spoke to the women who had gathered there'. And the lesson in the lesson, so to speak, both for a faith-and-culture class and for all those who have forgotten what it is the artists and writers are always telling us, is that Paul the far-seeing, Paul the pharisee, knew where the sacred hides most vividly: it has gone to ground 'outside the gate by the river'. It is ordinary and ordained, terrestrial yet extra-territorial, the solid ground and mainstream where we gossip and launder and drink water from the chalice of our hands. So the apostle to the Gentiles cues the continuing apostolate of writers and artists who get up and go to where the people gather in the consecrated thoroughfares, and who show them there and then in the here and now of a visible presentness, like the historic present of the Gospels when their eager Greek rushes into the immediacy of the indicative because everything is happening for the first time as we read it, that we are the glittering dialects of the Word of God and that this dialogue is the only worthwhile theology.

The Christian knows, or comes to know, that the Way and the Truth are not enough. Life too is needed. The artist and the writer know the same thing in another variety of Indo-European. They know that the Good and the True are not enough without the Beautiful and that the seraphim and the cherubim demonstrated thoroughbred taste when, according to Cyril of Alexandria, the archangelic courtiers of Paradise fell silent with a rapture far beyond their official duties as the filthy, impaled figure of Jesus of Nazareth walked among them. They had never seen anything more beautiful than this, the crisis of the human form.

When I was young, I visited Mount Athos. There on the holy Mountain, in a timeless Marian sanctuary, I tried to practise the skills of stillness. But when I ought to have been thinking of the realities beyond thought, of the unthinkable origin that is God, I was thoughtlessly deterred by the unimaginable continuum: on the knuckle of my hand, where my grandfather's signet ring could be argued off its finger only with cool cooking oil, a greenfly bent a bleached and individual follicle with his albino snorkel. And I was ashamed in myself of the first shoddy and headstrong cadences of Martha's Magnificat.

In the forests solitary men supplicated the Trinity. I walked through their broadleaf deserts to stay with idiorrhythmic monks and with cenobitic monks, and before I knew where I was I knew who I was: a boy with eyebrow pencil in a trainee moustache who wanted to explore the early chapters of a saint's life and not the later ones.

Accordingly, he lost and found himself in the same moment by returning to a village on the border which was called in demotic by the name Ouranopolis, the City of the World. Children were dancing under an awning there. The soles of their feet were streaked with broken ants. A fat old woman rested an accordion on her redundant bosoms, and played as if all life depended on it. Then a middle-aged man appeared from a butcher's shop beside her, his slaughtering apron slick with cartilage and bright goo; and high over his head, like some scroll of the Law from the ark of a synagogue, he held up a shiny fiddle.

I did not kiss him on the mouth and say: 'This at last is bone of my bones and flesh of my flesh'. I did not cling to him and tell him that he was everyman and any man; butcher, baker and candlestick-maker; predator, companion, and the melting instrument of God's light. I did not tell him that I wanted to live below the treeline, where exquisite species of flowers are pollinated by hideous insects, and not on the mountaintop where the wind would be the death of you. I did not think of saying that I had fallen in love with the annals of Hannah and with the woman who is accused, along with the apostles at Pentecost, of being in her cups when she is only raising the chalice; and I did not dream that she would become for me an emblem of freed speech, of love-cries beyond liturgy, of imagination at play and at work in the world.

Hannah invokes the God of hosts, Eli the God of Israel. So this summit of wise man and holy woman, of laity and clergy, brings together the twin images of the Almighty and the All Merciful, the fathering and the mothering metaphors of a mystery which tends and intends our childlike growth throughout our grown-up hoodlum adulthoods. As priest and poet bless each other, Logos and language greet each other in good-will, in longing and belonging, and the gorgeous, urgent dialogue springs up again. So let our artists freshen the telling of our tale. Let them fresco our oratories as they will stain our transparencies as they need to. Let them raise the roofs of our cathedrals and decant God's light. Let them teach us their Kyries, their Alleluias, their Amens, so that our Hosannas can become again Hannah's grand anthem.

My heart exults in the Lord, my strength is exalted in my God. The bows of the mighty are broken, but the feeble gird on strength. The Lord kills and brings to life; he brings down to Sheol and raises up. He raises up the poor from the dust; he lifts the needy from the ash heap, to make them sit with princes and inherit a seat of honour. For the pillars of the earth are the Lord's, and on them he has set the world.

WHERE IS THE OCEAN?

Bernadette McCarrick

What follows is spoken in the voice of a woman who is middle-aged, Christian, Catholic, and a member of an apostolic religious community.

Two hungers

We know from psychology that there are three basic strands in our hierarchy of human needs: physical, psychological and spiritual. I am aware as I write that I am warm and well-fed. That's the first need taken care of. Resting on that foundation is the need for relationship with others (communication), and built upon that, the need for relationship with the divine (spirituality). Our energies are constantly being devoted to the fulfilment of these three groups of needs. This article focuses on the manner in which we seek to satisfy the hunger for both communication and spirituality.

A question of awareness

Anthony de Mello tells a story about a little ocean fish who goes to an older, wiser fish to help him find this marvellous place everyone is talking about called The Ocean. If only he could find it! 'This is it,' said the older fish, doing a somersault in the water. 'You're actually swimming in it! We're all swimming in it!' 'Oh, this old place? This couldn't possibly be The Ocean!' said the little fish as he swam away disappointedly to look elsewhere. Wouldn't you just love to convince the foolish little creature of the futility of his search? I dare say it's not too difficult to realise that we find ourselves swimming in an ocean of communication every moment of the day. I hardly need to count the ways, from a simple hello to your neighbour to an e-mail to Down Under. But you don't need me to tell you that the stuff of communication is something far deeper and more personal. Sometimes we're in the role of the little fish, asking our questions, and at other times we're in the role of the older fish, providing the best answers we know. Yet, between us, currents of mutual disappointment flow. Never mind. I am sure that now and again two such fish are actually able to hear each other, and swim together for one shared moment in an ocean of joy. Of course all of us, from an early age, devote our energies to our interpersonal relationships and relatedness, thus causing ourselves to improve our communication skills, and many times arriving at mutually joyful moments which bring their own deep rewards. At such moments our basic need to be in relationship, to truly hear and be truly heard, is satisfied.

Soul
The third of our basic needs is the need to be in relationship with the divine. When do we feel this need? How do we fulfil it? To whom do we go with our questions? It seems that there are moments in life when we are particularly ripe for this journey; moments when we begin to speak the language of soul. When I was a child, in the late fifties and early sixties, my soul was an invisible but real whiteboard somewhere inside me. Small sins put small stains on it. Big sins put big stains. If I went to confession the whole board was wiped clean. But I had better not die with any stains on my soul.

Small stains would put me in purgatory. Big ones would put me you know where. It was all explained in catechism class.

Now that I am an adult, and with the benefit of much new thinking and writing, the word 'soul' evokes very different imagery for me: I am in my soul, surrounded by it, held together by it. My soul includes my body, with its physical needs. It includes my longing to love and be loved, which is fulfilled by good communication with other human beings. Yet my soul is so much more than that. No longer is it an imaginary whiteboard within me. Rather, it is the place where all my longings are lodged, especially my longing for relationship with the divine.

The books by the British psychotherapist Thomas Moore, *Care of the Soul* and *Soulmates*, made the bestseller list earlier in the nineties, as did our own John O'Donohue's *Anam Chara* of last year. This indicates widespread awareness and appreciation of soul, and that the word itself can now be spoken outside of a purely religious context and by more than so-called 'religious' voices. We owe a debt to Carl Jung for this new way of naming soul. It was Jung who discovered and described the collective unconscious which is composed of a number of archetypes. Among these are the Anima, a man's soul, and the Animus, a woman's spirit: two sides of the same coin. This spiritual blueprint, soul, is the matrix of religious expression. A moment of recognition comes in life when s/he acknowledges and nurtures the feeling that it brings up. And this is the time when many people enter the realm of spirituality and/or religion.

Spirituality
James McMahon, in *The Price of Wisdom,* says that spirituality is 'coming to grips with the reality that our

existence is a great mystery, and humbly accepting that'. Most people don't come to this point of awareness until a crisis awakens them to it. This usually takes the form of acute loss, such as the death of a loved one, or the loss of one's health or personal meaning. People learn to cope by cultivating an open mind about the mystery of life. This opening-of-mind can be nurtured by each individual according to his or her own tastes. For one it will be music, for another poetry, literature and the arts, for another hill-walking or paragliding. It is whatever helps people to remain open to the mystery that has visited their lives. McMahon further points out that spirituality takes us to where psychology cannot, yet psychology is necessary before spirituality can do that. In other words, the relationship with the divine rests on the foundation of human relationships.

Spirituality is not religion, however, and McMahon reminds us that many spiritual persons have no religious affiliation. This point is well illustrated by the contemporary poet and philosopher David Whyte in his poem 'Self Portrait'.

> It doesn't interest me if there is one God or many gods.
> I want to know if you belong or feel abandoned.
> If you know despair or can see it in others.[1]

Whyte seems to have placed his faith not in any religious doctrine, but in people's mutual care for one another, which is actually at the heart of communication.

My spirituality
I have many ways of holding open my own door to the

---

1. From *Fire in the Heart*, Many Rivers Meet Press, 1992.

mystery side of life. I lean a lot on poems and stories to provide images and words to help me deepen my understanding of the unfathomable. Two years ago I found a poem by Henry Taylor called 'Riding a One-Eyed Horse'.

> One side of his world is always missing.
> You may give it a casual wave of the hand,
> or rub it with your shoulder as you pass,
> but nothing on his blind side ever happens.
>
> Hundreds of trees slip past him into darkness
> drifting into a hollow hemisphere
> whose sounds you will have to try to explain.
> Your legs will tell him not to be afraid
> if you learn never to lie. Do not forget
> to turn his head, and let what comes come seen:
> he will jump the fences he has to if you swing
> toward them from the side that can see
>
> and hold his good eye straight. The heavy dark
> will stay beside you always: let him learn
> to lean against it. It will steady him
> and see you safely through diminished fields.

The title itself is enough for me at times. There are many levels of meaning in the poem. This poem reminds me that I cannot see everything; that there is a darkness which must be acknowledged and trusted; that I must travel gently and deliberately through life on my one-eyed horse. I never tire of reciting this poem to myself, and it continues to sustain me.

I have also been offered stories and texts to nourish my soul from Christian tradition and I constantly lean on them for meaning. For example, there was a time when people used to ask me why I was wasting my life 'locked up in a convent'. It was a challenging question which I respected at one level. Yet it angered me deeply. The implication seemed to be that I was wasting my womanhood in religious life, which could be better spent on husband and children. Years later I found the story in Mark's Gospel of an Unnamed Woman who anointed Jesus' head with that very expensive ointment. She was asked the same question: 'Why are you wasting all that preciousness?' Her questioners, like mine, seemed to imply that she was squandering a year's wages on an extravagance. This powerful metaphor from that woman's story has helped me to claim and love the mystery of my own celibacy.

Religion

According to James McMahon, 'religion is but one of the many ways that a person may choose to express spirituality. But it is not spirituality. As we all know, many folks involved with religion are far from spiritual'. Given that there are plenty of examples of this dichotomy, nevertheless there are many people whose spirituality best finds a home in the Christian tradition, in a Church whose faith is pledged both personally and communally to the Trinity and in particular to Christ himself. I am one of those people. How does this Church give me the nourishment I seek?

Personal experience of Church

The Catholic Church offers spiritual food to people through several channels: teachings, doctrines, liturgies, sacraments, sacred texts, pastoral presence and care, to name but some. Personally I look for nourishment in homily, ritual and in opportunities for pastoral sharing of my skills and gifts.

Homily: When I participate in the Eucharist, I long to be fed by the Liturgy of the Word as well as by the Liturgy of the Eucharist. My love for stories comes to the fore here. I remember best a six-minute homily which has a story for its centrepiece. Recently a priest in my local church began his homily with the words: 'McNulty's kitchen was a dark place….' I vividly remember the story, and the one point that it made I enjoyed very much.

Ritual: One of my most memorable experiences of Church occurred eight years ago in a small country church at the christening of my niece. Her parents named her Saraid, a name that means 'the best or noblest one' (as in the Gaelic 'Sár'). The extended family gathered in the little church. The ceremony progressed, and when it came to the Litany of the Saints, the priest added the name 'Saint Saraid'. 'Pray for us', we chorused back. I knew there was no Saint Saraid. Yet I was touched by this gesture on the part of the priest. Reflecting on it afterwards, I realised several things: the child was christening or Christianising the name by virtue of her bearing it. Warmth and informality were communicated to the whole family in the midst of the solemnity of the ritual. This was a sacrament not only of Baptism for Saraid, but a sacrament of inclusion and affirmation for her entire family. And still I have not fully fathomed what moved me so much in the sound of the words 'Saint Saraid'.

Pastoral opportunity
On Palm Sunday of this year, eighteen women met with me to reflect on the Gospel of the day. We focused on the story of Peter's denial. But this time we called out the character of the High Priest's Maid, and spent a while getting to know

her. We were fascinated by the woman we met. Re-naming her in our own language as The Priest's Housekeeper seemed to colour her character. By using our memories and imaginations we began to appreciate her daily life: her role in Peter's denial and her courage and integrity. We imagined that she followed Peter to wherever he went weeping; she cared for him in his brokenness in that moment. We went home convinced more than ever that the Word of God is certainly alive and active.

The meeting place

There are many places where communication and spirituality converge. One of the richest learnings of my life came from a lecturer I knew in Loyola University in Chicago. He taught us to do theology from good literature, mainly novels. I don't read many novels, but I try to apply this valuable learning to other art forms. Besides poetry, which I have mentioned already, I include films and plays. There are many of each which I never tire of revisiting because of their capacity to present to me the beauty of mystery, that mystery which is often in the Christian treasury of stories.

Film: About ten years ago, a Danish film called *Babette's Feast* came out. Babette, a cook, wins the lotto. As an act of appreciation to two elderly spinsters who had looked after her, she uses all the money to hold a feast in their home, to which she invites all the people in the local community. As they enjoy the excellent wine and course after course of Babette's sumptuous cooking, all their quarrels and grudges dissolve. And that's not all. I do not wish to spoil the reader's viewing by giving everything away. But I am sure anyone would agree that this classic work of art contains the best theology of the

Eucharist one could ever find. Another film, *Jesus of Montreal*, is a replay of the life of Jesus in modern times: a midrash which skilfully weaves together Jesus' story and our own. The best example of this takes place at the end of the film when Jesus is on the cross. The scene of the piercing of his side is like a scene from *ER*. The ambulance siren nee-naws as Jesus' heart is hastily harvested by a medical team, placed in a cooler, and rushed off to a patient awaiting a life-saving heart-transplant. 'Sacred Heart!', I kept saying to myself, as I watched that scene unfold, the word ringing with new meaning.

Theatre: Recently, on reading Sebastian Barry's award-winning play *The Steward of Christendom*, I was taken by the final speech. It is the story of a man, his young son, and their dog Shep. Shep had committed the crime of devouring a precious ewe. Father and son agreed that Shep should be hung. But the little boy, because he loved the dog so sorely, could not bear the thought of it, and he and Shep spent the night in the cold wood nearby, afraid to come home, driving the father to distraction with worry. When dawn came, the searching neighbours brought home the boy and Shep, both of whom now felt they were for the slaughter. The boy concludes the story: 'My feet carried me on to where [my father] stood, immortal you would say, in the door. And he put his right hand on the back of my head, and pulled me to him so that my cheek rested against the buckle of his belt. And he raised his own face to the brightening sky and praised someone, in a crushed voice, God maybe, for my safety, and stroked my head. And the dog's crime was never spoken of, but that he lived till he died. And I would call that the mercy of fathers, when the love that lies in them deeply like the glittering face of a well is betrayed by an emergency, and the child sees at last that he is loved, loved and needed and not to be lived without, and greatly.'[2]

I have shared this story with a friend who was hurt and worried about the behaviour of his young son. He found consolation in it. In my community, we used this story for prayer. It seems to us a salvation story, one that echoes other sacred stories both from the scriptures and from our own lives. Presented through theatre as an art form, this beautiful story holds together the most vital energies of both communication and spirituality.

Conclusion

There is only one Ocean. This environment in which we 'live and move and have our being' is teeming with the many facets of communication between us humans. This same environment is also teeming with a divine presence to which, at one moment or another in life, we find ourselves wanting to respond. There are many ways in which we acknowledge that hunger and seek to nourish it. All I can do in this short article is to say how and where I find my sustenance. The longing continues alongside the many moments of fulfilment.

2.   *The Steward of Christendom*, London: Methuen, 1995.

CHRISTIANITY AND THE ARTS

John Moriarty

Quite a few years ago now I was in London and I was desolate and not a little alienated from what was going on all around me. How in God's name, I was wondering, can people give themselves to this kind of life, and, since they so obviously do, what is this saying about us as a species? Needing to come into contact with another and maybe a more hopeful estimation of ourselves, I emerged from the Underground and crossed into Westminster Abbey. I was only still getting used to the great, great emptiness of the place when it was announced over the intercom that a eucharistic rite would shortly be celebrated in St George's chapel immediately to the right, aside the main entrance. Aware that I was a Catholic and that I hadn't much regard for dragon slayers, I nonetheless retraced my steps, pushed open the glass doors and sat in what turned out to be a very small side-chapel, waiting. In all there were six of us in the congregation. I was happily surprised to see, when he entered, how splendidly, if simply, attired the minister was. He greeted us and proceeded. Again now I was surprised, happily so, by the great dignities, gestural and verbal, of the rite.

We prayed in unison:

> Almighty God, Our Heavenly Father,
> We have sinned against you and against
> Our fellow men

In thought and word and deed,
Through negligence, through weakness,
Through our own deliberate fault.
We are truly sorry,
And repent of all our sins.
For the sake of your son Jesus Christ,
Who died for us,
Forgive us all that is past
And grant that we may serve you in
Newness of life
To the glory of your name.
Amen.

Facing us, his hands outstretched, the minister prayed that God would pardon us:

May Almighty God
Who forgives all who truly repent
Have mercy upon you,
Pardon and deliver you from all your sins,
Confirm and strengthen you in all goodness
And keep you in life eternal
Through Jesus Christ our Lord.
Amen.

We recited the Gloria:

Glory to God in the highest and peace to his people on
earth.
Lord God, heavenly King, Almighty God and Father,
We worship you, we give you thanks, we praise you for
you glory.

Lord Jesus Christ, only son of the Father,
Lord God, Lamb of God,
Have mercy on us;
You are seated at the right hand of the Father, receive
    our prayer.
For you alone are the Holy One,
You alone are the Lord,
You alone are the most high,
Jesus Christ,
With the Holy Spirit,
In the glory of God the Father.
Amen.

Continuing in this guise, with unaffected, calm dignity, we crossed into what I, a Catholic, would call the canon of the Mass.

Sitting as I was quite close to the altar, I heard the sound of the host being broken. And then, from the side of the altar, I heard the drip, drip, drip, drop, drop of the water flowing into the wine.

And now I found myself asking a question: these sounds I have just heard – are they not, for a Christian, the most serious sounds in the universe? With or without theological justification, I thought of them as the sounds of the universe being redeemed, as the sounds of the universe turning back towards its Divine Source. And Christ undergoing his passion and death and resurrection is the agonised hinge upon which it is turning.

They are simple sounds:

The sound of bread being broken.
The sound of water being poured into wine.

Sounds as serious as the sound of God's voice calling the universe into existence. Sounds as serious as the sound of God's voice revealing his will on Mount Sinai. Sounds as serious as the sound of the 'Tuba Mirum' on the last day.

> Tuba mirum spargens sonum
> per sepulchra regionum
> coget omnes ante thronum

And since my theme is the Church and the arts, may I say this: we should liturgically see to it that these sounds will be heard in their awe-ful, unadorned simplicity. To script them and score them in the way that Bach might or Handel might or Mozart might or Verdi might would be to assuage them in their terribleness. Their terribleness we must never take from them.

This does not mean that we should banish the arts from the liturgy and from the Church. Not at all. What I'm attempting to say is this. There is a sanctum, liturgical and architectural, into which the arts may not go. Indeed, there is a boundary they cannot and will not and may not overpass, not because the God who spoke to Job out of the whirlwind confronts them at that boundary, saying, 'thus far shalt thou come and no farther', but because this boundary is in itself their natural limit. Beyond it they lose their power not just to embody the Mysterium *tremendum et fascinans*, they lose their power even to point in its direction. To say of the Mystery that it is tremendous and fascinating is already to have gone too far.

The Tao Te Ching tells us that:

> The Tao that can be spoken isn't the Tao.

It further tells us that:

> He who speaks does not know.
> He who knows does not speak.

I am not questioning the right of art to its hallowed, ancient role in the liturgy and in the Church. I am seeking only to determine its limits.

Take the talk about 'the aesthetic experience'. Like so many of our learned words, the word 'aesthetic' is of Greek origin. Taken at its most comprehensive, the Greek word *aisthesis* means sensory awareness. Now, it is virtually a truism of mystical instruction that we must go beyond the senses, and this surely implies that if we are to reach our goal, which is union with God, then we mustn't forever malinger in the lesser beneficence of aesthetic experience. Listen to St John of the Cross:

> O wretched condition of this life wherein it is so dangerous to live and so difficult to find the truth. That which is most clear and true is to us most obscure and doubtful and we therefore avoid it though it is most necessary for us. That which shines the most and dazzles our eyes, that we embrace and follow after though it is most hurtful to us and makes us stumble at every stop. In what fear and danger then must man be living seeing that the very light of his natural eyes by which he directs his steps is the very first to bewilder and deceive him when he would draw near unto God. If he wishes to be sure of the road he travels on he must close his eyes and walk in the dark if he is to journey in safety from his domestic foes which are his own senses and faculties.

The Kena Upanishad is classically imperturbable:

> There goes neither the eye nor speech nor the mind; we
> know it not; nor do we see how to teach one about it.
> Different it is from all that is known, and beyond the
> unknown it also is.

Its as if the Upanishad was saying, there goes neither
Gregorian chant, nor the rose windows of Gothic
Christendom, nor the glories of the Sistine ceiling, nor the
arias of the *Messiah*.

Astonishingly, D. H. Lawrence would agree:

> *The Hills*
> I lift mine eyes unto the hills
> And there they are, but no strength comes from them
>   to me.
> Only from darkness
> Only from darkness
> And ceasing to see
> Strength comes.

> *Travel is over*
> I have travelled and looked at the world and loved it.
> Now I don't want to look at the world any more,
> There seems nothing there.
> In not looking, and not-seeing
> Comes a new strength
> And undeniable new Gods share their life with us when
> we cease to see.

These poems can be read as arguments for Tenebrae, the

ritual in which Christians cross into the darkness of Good Friday.

In Tenebrae we aren't bathed in the light or soothed by the sounds of our own creations.

Tenebrae is meta-aesthetic.

Tauler tells us that when St Paul saw nothing he saw God.

Maybe I've said enough to make my point. But do please remember that what I've been saying is not an argument for iconoclasm. On the contrary. What we see in a church should, if possible, be even more beautiful than what we might expect to see in an art gallery. What we hear in a church should, if possible, be even more beautiful than what we might expect to hear in a concert hall. After all, the mystic who talked so elaborately about the dark night of the senses and the dark night of the soul is himself among the greatest poets in the Spanish language. There is heavenly medicine in a Rublev icon. And I'm not so sure that $E=mc^2$ would not feel a need to veil its face in the presence of some Zen drawings. Those drawings are then greater revelations of how things are. Times there are when we feel like saying to a Mozart andante: into thy hands for now I commend my spirit.

And yet, the limits of art are not the limits of the seeking soul. Art at its term is not the seeking soul at its term.

> In not looking, and not-seeing
> Comes a new strength
> And undeniable new Gods share their life with us when
> we cease to see.

But as Zen Buddhists remind us: first there is a mountain, then there is no mountain, then again there is a mountain. And when, after absorption in the Divine, we once again open our eyes and look at the mountain, we know the seeing we know, that the seeing and the mountain we see aren't more than the Divine we have, yet haven't emerged from.

It is when we reach home that we come to know we never left home.

O diclosa ventura.

POST-MODERN IRELAND –
A CHRISTIAN RESPONSE

Eamonn Conway

Introduction

In a recent article on faith and culture, Michael Paul Gallagher SJ called for 'a post-modernity of our own Christian making, an energetic seizing of the moment'.[1] At first glance this might seem quite strange. Do we not associate modernity and post-modernity with everything that is opposed to Christianity? Have we not seen the decay of Christian faith in most modern and post-modern societies? How could we have a post-modernity of our own Christian making?

At the same time Christianity is understood to be incarnational. This means that at each moment in history the story of God and humanity as told by the life of Jesus Christ and remembered by the Christian community is meant to take flesh and come alive in a fresh and life-giving way. Faced with the questions and the concerns of each new culture, the Christian community is to be 'like a householder who brings out from his storeroom things both old and new'.[2] There is a

---

1. 'Post-modernity: Friend or foe'. In Eoin Cassidy (ed.), *Faith and Culture in the Irish Context*, Dublin: Veritas, 1996, p. 81. Prof Gallagher develops his argument in *Clashing Symbols – An Introduction to Faith and Culture*, London: Darton Longman and Todd, 1997.
2. Matthew 13:52.

richness in this image of the Christian tradition as a storeroom of old and new treasures. There are treasures that are old yet valuable because the fundamental hungers of the human heart do not change from one generation to the next. There are also new treasures: each moment in history, as it brings new problems and opportunities, unfolds hidden and unsuspected resources in the Christian tradition. The Christian tradition needs these new problems, questions and opportunities to keep it alive, to energise and replenish its treasure-house of faith.

What follows is an attempt to assess some of the issues confronting the Christian tradition in the context of contemporary Ireland and then to visit the storeroom of Christian faith with a view to formulating 'a post-modernity of our own Christian making'.

Is Ireland post-modern?

The first point that must be addressed is whether or not contemporary Ireland may be described as 'post-modern'. To some extent this depends on what is meant by the term. Without going into further debate here I will accept Gallagher's description of intellectual post-modernity as characterised by a suspicion of reason, of naive claims to progress, of utopian perspectives on history; by a sense of loneliness and loss of connections; finally, by a continuity with modernity in terms of the primacy afforded to subjective personal experience. The legacy of modernity, according to Gallagher, is fragmentation of the sense of self, of the sense of truth, and of the sense of God. However, there are signs that cultural post-modernity, because it includes 'a humbler recognition of wounds and wants' can signal the opening of doors to spiritual enquiry previously slammed shut by a modernity that was more arrogant and self-contained.[3]

To what extent could this description of post-modernity reflect a dominant mood in contemporary Irish society?

The Celtic Tiger: more than an economic boom

At the moment it is counter-cultural to speak negatively of developments in Ireland. Ireland is the proud home of the Celtic Tiger. Though two-thirds of the population say they personally have not experienced its benefits, few doubt its existence.[4] Strictly speaking the Celtic Tiger refers to the current economic boom. However, it has also become short-hand for a country that is perceived as less stuffy and more tolerant, 'vibrant and outward-looking, willing to absorb many influences and listen to many voices'.[5] Developments have been helped along by the destruction (because of scandals one might say the self-destruction) of the Catholic Church's authority. The Church's influence is now widely perceived, even by many of its members who have remained faithful, to have had a stifling effect on personal freedom and social progress.

There is also a new confidence about resolving problems in Northern Ireland. This has been marked by a growing intolerance of intransigent positions which seem, in an open and liberal society, bigoted, dogmatic and rooted in old quarrels which no longer have any relevance or importance.

---

3. Gallagher, op. cit., pp. 75-77.
4. Cf. John Waters, *An Intelligent Person's Guide to Modern Ireland*, London: Duckworth, 1997, p. 8. Waters compares belief in the 'miracle' of the Celtic Tiger to acceptance of the authenticity of the Marian apparitions at Knock a century previously.
5. Fergal Keane, *Letter to Daniel – Despatches from the Heart*, London: Penguin, 1996, p. 221.

As Ireland prepares to take a front seat in the Europe of the twenty-first century, Republicans in balaclavas and Orangemen in bowler hats are increasingly perceived as primitive and embarrassing anachronisms.

So at first glance the news would seem good. But have all the developments been bought at a high price? There is another side to the story.

Lives of quiet desperation

Let's take as an example the extraordinarily high suicide rate in Ireland at the present time. It is estimated that half a dozen (mainly young) males commit suicide each week. A hospital sister told me that in one regional hospital alone, five to seven people are admitted each day who have attempted to end their lives. Rarely do we find that it is people on the predictable margins who are attempting to kill themselves; the people we see begging on bridges or taking drugs in derelict buildings. Those who commit suicide usually take the community by surprise. In the wake of a suicide the comments are familiar: he had everything going for him; she had recently got a place in college or a promotion at work; he was a leading member of the local football team.

The people who commit suicide would seem to have been 'leading lives of quiet desperation' (Thoreau). On the surface everything seemed well; beneath the surface there must have been a very different sense of unrecognised isolation and loneliness, hidden pain and despair. Recently I attended a Leaving Certificate graduation ceremony at my home school. Everyone, including myself, was telling these school-leavers that the world was their oyster. We kept telling them that they had no grounds for fear, no reason to have any self-doubts. They could stand with their heads held high among the best of their generation in Europe. As I watched each of these Leaving Certificate students confidently embrace the microphone and express words of gratitude or of hope for the future, I couldn't help contrast it with how I believe most of my class felt leaving school hardly twenty years ago, with many fears and doubts, wondering if we could make it, not expecting much of ourselves and unsure if others expected much of us either. This new confidence among present school-leavers is to be welcomed, and yet I wonder if it bears with it a great pressure, and this in a number of ways. First of all, the pressure to perform and to succeed. From those who have, more is expected. If the world is your oyster then you have no one to blame but yourself if things do not work out well. Second, what if school-leavers only seem confident but actually have hidden doubts and fears? How free are they to express their worries about the future? Are they not under peer pressure to keep up the appearance, in the words of the Simon and Garfunkel song, 'to play the game and pretend'? And are they not also perhaps under unacknowledged pressure from their parents who are proud to see their sons and daughters less inhibited and more confident than themselves; with knowledge, skills and attitudes they themselves never dreamed of possessing?

Ill-equipped for the pain of living

I question if young people today, despite their knowledge, freedom and opportunity, are being equipped to cope with the pain, struggle and general messiness that is part and parcel of any human life in any time and place. What is more, I believe that the message they hear from many voices in society is that a life free of such messiness is not only possible but theirs for the asking. This means that when pain and messiness come they are unexpected and leave young people all the more vulnerable and confused. Little wonder, then, that they are devastated when a relationship does not work out, when a job is more than they can handle, or when they encounter failure in one form or another. Paul Murray, in his poem 'A note on human passion', writes:

> ...one must not anaesthetise
> or dull the pain
> but instead sustain
> the splintered heart's
> helpless yet terrifying
> and sharp desire
> never to be healed
> of the wound of living...[6]

Obviously people who are addicted to drugs of different kinds are attempting to anaesthetise the pain of living. But any form of behaviour which compels people to give their energy to things that are not their true desires is also an addiction.[7] Work, shaping one's career, the acquisition of money or property, expensive and often dangerous pastimes, relationships which are more about dependency than friendship, all of these can be addictions. Just to comment on the first of these: work. Today, many people become identified entirely with their work and virtually disappear behind it. Perhaps Celtic Tiger booms only come about when people do. But are we taking account of the cost in human terms? The danger of addictive lifestyles, of whatever kind, is that gradually they erode the capacity for depth.

---

6. In *The Absent Fountain*, Dublin: Dedalus Press, 1991, p. 28.
7. Cf. Gerald May, *Addiction and Grace*, London: HarperCollins, 1988, p. 14.

Not everyone may take the path of addiction. Instead some lower their horizons, accept that this is the way life is, and settle for 'half-living their lives, half-dreaming their dreams, half-loving their loves, becoming half-people' (Brendan Kennelly). They avoid despair by converting their disappointment into 'a courageous and self-limiting fortitude'.[8]

A sense of dislocation and loss of identity

For some time now I have been puzzled and concerned about the apparent lack of a sense of history among third-level students. Events that lie outside their immediate experience, whether they happened just before they were born or centuries ago, seem totally irrelevant to them. It is not as though they were afraid of history: it is as if they lacked a category by which to consider past events. This sense of disconnectedness from the past, and puzzlement as to why it should matter, have no doubt contributed positively to moving the peace process in the North of Ireland along, where, for centuries, old battles fuelled new sources of division. Now, an increasing number of young adults in the North want to get on with life, seek their identity in a new Europe, and benefit to the full from the economic prosperity that an end to violence may ensure.

At the same time, this lack of a sense of history, this 'cheerful ahistoricality', as Paul Lakeland calls it, represents a tremendous impoverishment. It means that the present generation must virtually invent itself. It has no background, no personal story to unite and inspire, nothing to locate it in a context wider and greater than itself. To use an analogy:

---

8. Cf. Paul Lakeland, *Postmodernity – Christian identity in a fragmented age*, Minneapolis: Augsburg Press, 1997, p. 9.

children who are adopted sometimes find it hard to live without knowledge of their birth-parents and family background. Pieces of the jigsaw essential to their personal identity and self-worth are missing. When they are unable to find the missing pieces, it can sometimes be very difficult to compensate for the loss. Similarly, a generation that has become separated from its own personal history is cut off from an essential aspect of its identity and source of self-worth, and here too the result can be detrimental and destructive.

The contemporary sense of disconnectedness is not only from the past: it is also from many aspects of the present. I am amazed how, for example, the scandals in the Church have passed so many young people completely by. Young adults may be disaffected, but it is not because of a sense of outrage at what Church representatives have done. The outrage comes more from older people who themselves feel hurt or let down by an institutional Church they once looked up to. For an increasing number of younger people the Church is not even a source of disappointment: it is simply not a part of their world at all. Their world is that of MTV and the Worldwide Web, and maybe the sports pages of the tabloids. In general, their level of interest in and knowledge of current affairs is appallingly low. Reality, whatever form it takes, simply does not sell. Anything which encourages fantasies is bound to be a success. Steadily the real world shrinks from view and a virtual world replaces it. Virtual reality is attractive because people can create these artificial worlds for themselves and therefore be gods in their own universe. They are in control and can feel secure. In virtual reality, people can hide behind assumed identities and practise an economy of self-disclosure. There, they may be alone, but at least they feel safe.

There is yet a third form of disconnectedness. This is from any sense of place. People move around more than ever before. This may be because of their work: increasingly people are employed in companies with multinational interests. Further, information technology means that many people can live and work wherever they like, at home, in the car or overseas. But aside from the requirements of their jobs people seem to have a need to be on the move; to be somewhere else; not to remain too long where they are now. There is a reluctance to form community, to get to know neighbours, to become involved in a locality. Thus people may live in a so-called 'dormer' town, drive to work, and spend the weekends socialising somewhere else. We have not yet even begun to reckon with the implications of this in terms of Church, to which the concept of community is so vital and central.

The task: self-invention, not self-discovery

Recently, speaking at a seminar on Christian discipleship, I quoted Frederick Buechner's description of a vocation as 'the place where your deepest gladness and the world's deepest hunger meet'. In response, one man in his mid-twenties said that he felt there was nothing in life he could do that would be uniquely and distinctively his contribution. He felt his life was utterly replaceable and disposable. If he stopped doing what he was doing, somebody else would simply take his place. The issue here was the absence of a unique sense of personal identity and self-worth.

If identity is no longer seen as a weapon or as a symbol of exclusion,[9] this is a welcome change, but again it has been bought at a high price. Identity is no longer a weapon because it is too weak to be used as one. Disconnectedness both from

9. Loc. cit.

past and present realities, as well as the loss of a sense of place, mean that personal identity is fragile and brittle. This is why people are so quick to adopt surrogate identities offered to them, whether by designer clothing, fashion and pop culture, or fundamentalist religious and political movements. These help to postpone facing the painful reality that, as Jean-Paul Sartre said:

> For human reality, to be is to choose oneself; nothing comes to it either from the outside or from within which it can receive or accept. Without any help whatsoever, it is entirely abandoned to the intolerable necessity of making itself be – down to the slightest detail.[10]

People see their task today as one not of self-discovery but self-invention. The implication is that we are nothing at birth. Culture is all, nature and inheritance little. We are who we become through our own efforts. We are what we achieve. To give up on achieving, performing, succeeding, would be to give up on life itself. We are free to make something of ourselves, but in a sense our freedom is a burden. We are, as Sartre put it, 'condemned to be free'.

The post-modern search for spiritual meaning

To return, then, to the opening question. The evidence is mounting that in a number of respects contemporary Irish society fits in with the post-modern picture. However, one aspect remains to be examined. Modernity heralded the death of God, and with it, the end of religion. In contrast, post-

---

10. Jean-Paul Sartre, *Being and Nothingness* (trans. Barnes), London: Methuen, 1958, pp. 440-441, cited in Nicholas Lash, *The Beginning and the End of Religion*, Cambridge: Cambridge University Press, 1996, p. 239.

modernity is marked by an openness, if not to God or religion, at least to spirituality. Do we find such an openness in Ireland at the present time? There is ample evidence that a post-modern spiritual search is well under way in Ireland. What characterises this search as post-modern is its suspicion of the intellect, rejection of institutions, resistance to structure, and emphasis on personal and subjective experience. It is also marked by a kind of 'cherry-picking' approach to the various world religions and traditions.

A glance at any issue of *Intercom* shows what 'sells' in Irish religious circles today: 'Meeting the God within through his(!) manifestation in nature', 'Discovering the inner rainbow', 'Dancing your story', 'Healing touch – therapeutic touch', and, of course, 'Celtic Spirituality'. What is ironic is that many of these courses and programmes have become the bread and butter of former seminaries and religious houses throughout the country.

One very obvious sign of the extent of the post-modern search for spiritual meaning is the recent extraordinary success of John O'Donohue's *Anam Chara*.[11] This book dove-tails perfectly with the post-modern search for meaning. It draws widely on the various religious traditions and gurus: Buddhism, Pablo Neruda, Meister Eckhart, Zen, the Kalyani-Mitra, the Native Americans, Hegel. Celtic myths and stories also get a mention but not nearly enough to merit the subtitle to the book: 'spiritual wisdom from the Celtic world'. Little is said about Jesus Christ, nothing at all about Church. There are lengthy reflections on love but these focus more on its benefits than its cost. Nicholas Lash alerts us to the subtle danger of this kind of spirituality:

11. John O'Donohue, *Anam Chara. Spiritual Wisdom from the Celtic World*, London: Bantam Press, 1997.

My mistrust of contemporary interest in 'spirituality' arises from the suspicion that quite a lot of material set out in bookstores under this description sells because it does not stretch the mind or challenge our behaviour. It tends to soothe rather than subvert our well-heeled complacency.[12]

The problem with much of contemporary spirituality is precisely as Lash suggests: it supports rather than challenges our post-modern lifestyles. It does not necessarily call any of our values or attitudes into question. It cannot, because this kind of spirituality is itself the product of a directionless post-modernity and thus can only be a coping mechanism for survival within it.

*

It would seem from what has been said so far that Ireland is well on its way to being a post-modern society, with all the accompanying sense of disorientation, disconnectedness and fragmentation that characterises such societies. The question we must now examine is which treasures in the storeroom of Christian faith can uplift us at this lonely moment in our journey through history.

---

12. Nicholas Lash, op.cit., p. 174. Writing on the same subject Hans Urs von Balthasar says: 'Outside the Christian domain the most important religious phenomenon appears to be an urgent and often desperate desire to flee from the senseless merry-go-round of technical civilisation to a transcendental sphere of peace. It doesn't seem to matter whether this sphere is God's or the seeker's own self or something neutral in between' ('Christian Prayer', *Communio*, 5, 1978, p. 16).

Sweeping away the debris

Before moving to a more theoretical reflection on the Christian story, a few practical comments must be made.

We have already noted that the post-modern mindset remains very suspicious of institution and structure. Thus, even aside from the various scandals, the institutional Church has a serious credibility problem. Fewer people are looking to the Church for leadership, and this includes in spiritual matters. Important statements and documents no longer attract even negative comment. Vocations to priesthood and religious life are dwindling rapidly, in quality as well as quantity, yet almost all positions of responsibility in the Church remain in the hands of ordained clergy. By international standards there is still an unusually high Church practice rate in Ireland, but the increasing absence of young people on a regular basis is significant.

Paradoxically, and in this regard Ireland may well be unique among post-modern countries, many people, young and old, remain passionately committed to the Church, but their voices are largely unheard and their energy and their enthusiasm remain untapped. Many of these are women, both lay and in religious life, and it remains to be seen just how long they will stand waiting on the sidelines.

The questions which those in Church leadership must now explore are: what changes in structures and institutions are necessary if the Church is to proclaim faithfully and effectively the Good News in a post-modern culture? What changes are necessary so that freshness, liveliness and enthusiasm are restored to the proclamation and the celebration of the Good News? The proclamation of the Good News is the Church's mission. The danger is that it would substitute for this mission, loyalty to outmoded forms and structures of ministry. To remain faithful, the Church has no choice but to change. Structures are not ends in themselves: they are merely the particular forms which the mission of the Church takes as it journeys through history.

The Church would seem to be crumbling in post-modern Ireland. But as the debris is swept away we realise that little of the edifices which have collapsed were essential to its proclamation of the Good News. In fact, without them, and with a healthy dose of creativity and imagination, the Church might prove to be in far better condition, leaner and healthier, to speak the words of compassion, healing and forgiveness which it uniquely is authorised and commissioned to do.

With this in mind, we will now see if we can find some such words which might find an echo in the post-modern search for meaning.

From the death of God to God's burial

Modernity accepted that humanity had no need of God. It could stand on its own two feet. Not only that, modernity also understood belief in God to be an impediment to humanity exercising its freedom fully and assuming full responsibility for itself. Modernity therefore announced the death of God. Theologians such as Jürgen Moltmann responded by focusing on the crucifixion of Jesus Christ, seeing in this a moment when modernity's cry of 'the death of God' takes on a whole new meaning.[13] Here, on the cross, is God, through Jesus, identifying with humanity even in its experience of utter Godforsakenness. Moltmann was making the point that no human experience, not even modernity's experience of the absence of God, is foreign or alien to God.

---

13. Cf. Jürgen Moltmann, *The Crucified God*, London: SCM, 1974.

Post-modernity is gone beyond proclaiming the death of God. God's apparent absence is now readily accepted; it is no longer news. People get on with enduring their lives of quiet desperation. Some sink themselves in endless activity and noise. Others accept that the death of God signals the disappearance of any ultimate meaning or significance to their lives, and stoically 'suffer the slings and arrows of outrageous fortune'.

In terms of the Christian story the post-modern moment in history corresponds not to the death of Jesus on the cross, but to his burial; to those dark hours when Jesus lay in the tomb. Each Easter we gloss over these important hours so quickly. We miss the point of the non-liturgy on Holy Saturday; the stripping bare of the altars and the awkward and eerie silence. The scriptures themselves have little to say regarding the burial of Jesus. In John's highly symbolic account, however, we note a few interesting points. We find, for example, that it is two strangers who come to retrieve the body.[14] Peter and the others are nowhere to be found; they are either locked in an upper room, gone to Emmaus or gone back to their fishing nets as if nothing has happened. It is two hitherto secret disciples of Jesus, Nicodemus, who first visited Jesus at night, and Joseph of Arimathea, who become the custodians of Jesus' remains. And it is a woman, Mary of Magdala, who is the first to visit the tomb, significantly, while it is still dark.[15]

An energetic seizing of the moment
It would seem that, at the moment of the death and burial of

---

14. Cf. John 19: 38-42.
15. Cf. John 20:1.

Jesus, the stage belonged not to the principal actors, but to those who, up until now, had played insignificant walk-on parts and who had been mainly observing from the wings. Nicodemus hardly counts as a disciple at all: he is described as a Pharisee, a leader among the Jewish (and therefore unbelieving) people. In John's Gospel he represents the educated yet critical and somewhat sceptical enquirer.[16] Neither could Mary of Magdala, who, we are told, had seven demons exorcised from her by Jesus, be considered a leading light among the disciples.[17]

Is 'an energetic seizing of the moment' in response to the post-modern sense of loss and disorientation possible? At the moment in the Christian story when loss was most keenly experienced we find that the energy comes not from those most readily identified with the story, but from people who have been lurking on the perimeters. Could this be telling us that we need to listen to those on the edges today; to novelists, artists and musicians, scientists and social-workers; to the many sometimes critical voices who evidently remain captivated by the Christ-event, but who, whether like Nicodemus out of scepticism, or Joseph of Arimathea out of fear, are unwilling to become explicitly identified with Christianity?

He descended into hell

There is one further aspect of the death and burial of Jesus to consider. What happens to Jesus during this dark night between burial and resurrection? The Apostles' Creed answers this question with the often neglected line 'he descended to the dead',

---

16. Cf. John 3:1-21.
17. Cf. Mark 16:9; Luke 8:2.

or, in the more traditional translation, 'he descended to hell'. Hell, we understand, is the place of eternal punishment for those who have refused God's love. What was Jesus doing in hell?

In recent times Hans Urs von Balthasar has considered this question.[18] He sees in Jesus' descent to hell God's clear message that no matter how we try, we cannot put ourselves outside the range of God's love.

Those in hell have freely chosen to reject all love; they have sought absolute loneliness. God wishes to respect their freedom yet at the same time let them know that their choice has not diminished God's love for them. As a last gesture of love, therefore, God 'sends' Jesus to hell. God allows Jesus to become one of them; to experience all they experience, even to share their sense of being cut off and abandoned. Jesus appears before them as one of themselves. He is not pretending to go through what they are going through: he actually goes through it. This means that hell, the state of utter abandonment, loneliness and desolation, is no longer outside God's loving presence.[19] Thus the lines of the psalm take on a whole new significance:

> Where could I go to escape your spirit?
> Where could I flee from your presence?
> If I climb the heavens, you are there,
> there too, if I lie in Sheol.[20]

But God's presence in this most desolate of places becomes possible only by Jesus surrendering everything: authority,

---

18. Hans Urs von Balthasar, *The von Balthasar Reader*, Edinburgh: T&T Clark, 1982, p. 153.
19. Op. cit., pp. 421-422.
20. Psalm 139:7-8.

power, life itself. It becomes possible because Jesus is prepared to share fully the sense of desolation and Godforsakeness of those in hell. Only by Jesus so doing is their state of abandonment brought within the reach of God's love.

Post-modernity: strength in weakness

In Jesus' descent to hell we have a moment in the Christian story that corresponds to the post-modern sense of loneliness and desolation. There is Good News here for people whose life experience is a 'living hell'. Though their experience is one of abandonment and Godforsakeness, the Good News is that they are not abandoned or forsaken. They have not and they cannot put themselves outside the reach of God's love.

There is only one way for the Christian community to communicate this message. It must become at one with those who experience abandonment and desolation. It must itself become abandoned and desolate. When we pause for a moment to consider it, this is exactly what is happening the Church today. The Church is experiencing abandonment, loneliness, isolation, desolation. And perhaps there is a divine economy in this. Because of it, the Church can both reach and redeem the loneliness and desolation of the post-modern age.

Conclusion

This article has attempted to sketch a post-modernity of our own Christian making. It has attempted to discover in the Christian story something that corresponds to the moment in history in which we find ourselves. It would be nice to end this article with a reference to the resurrection. But that might console us prematurely and anticipate a moment in history which is yet to come. For the present perhaps the

most appropriate stance is summed up in these lines from
T.S. Eliot's 'East Coker':

> I said to my soul, be still, and let the dark come upon
>   you
> Which shall be the darkness of God. As, in a theatre,
> The lights are extinguished, for the scene to be changed
> With a hollow rumble of wings, with a movement of
>   darkness on darkness,
> And we know that the hills and the trees, the distant
>   panorama
> And the bold imposing façade are all being rolled away –
> … I said to my soul, be still, and wait without hope
> For hope would be hope for the wrong thing; wait
>   without love
> For love would be love of the wrong thing; there is yet
>   faith
> But the faith and the love and the hope are all in the
>   waiting.
> Wait without thought, for you are not ready for
>   thought:
> So the darkness shall be the light, and the stillness the
>   dancing.[18]

---

18. 'East Coker' from *Four Quartets*, London: Faber&Faber Ltd.

PRAYER

Dermot Bolger

I have come this long way without finding you
Or losing your reflection,

I've tried a dozen obsessions without cleansing
Your taste from my tongue.

Oldest friend and adversary, fugitive brother,
We recognise each other

In carriages of express trains which pass:
Your hands beat on the glass.

OLD YARNS AND NEW STORIES

Thomas Casey SJ

Introduction

In his book *Inventing Ireland: The Literature of a Modern Nation*, Declan Kiberd recounts a delightful incident originally told by Tomás Ó Criomhtháinn. A group of Blasket Islanders were given the fateful news of the rebellion of Easter 1916 up in Dublin. Ó Criomhtháinn invited them to say the word 'republic' in Irish: 'Abair an focal *republic* i nGaoluinn'.[1] However, they had no word for 'republic', a fact which did not unduly bother them. Ó Criomhtháinn gently rebuked them, saying 'Agus is beag a chuir a soláthar imní ach oiread oraibh'[2]. (And it's little its acquisition worried ye for that matter.)

People from today's Republic of Ireland are in an analogous situation with regard to the Catholic Church. Its Easter message does not translate into the language of our everyday experience. And we are not losing much sleep over it. We are witnessing the collapse of a larger-than-life story we once cherished and people are not rushing to lament its passing. Many are wishing it good riddance.

There is something post-modern about this rejection of big stories. Not that I want to claim Ireland as an unambiguously

---

1. Declan Kiberd, *Inventing Ireland: The Literature of a Modern Nation*, London: Jonathan Cape, 1995, p. 286.
2. Ibid.

post-modern society. I believe it is more a fast-moving whirl of the modern and post-modern. Our social landscape is rapidly changing, our sense of what it means to be human is on the move, and yet there is a tremendous confidence and buoyancy underlying all this transformation. The expanding economy has created a feel-good factor and our new-found faith in ourselves is exorcising a cloying religious superstition. However, even though we are confidently modern, there is the vague sense that we are accelerating into something unknown which is more than modernity. We are not sure what it will be. Perhaps we will happily arrive at the full flowering of everything we now celebrate. Maybe it will involve a more balanced appraisal of the pluses and minuses of the nineties. We might even wake up to discover that we are no longer in Disneyland.

In his book *The Postmodern Condition*, the French philosopher Jean-François Lyotard[3] takes the fashionable and confusing term 'post-modern' to mean incredulity about the big stories or meta-narratives in our culture. He writes of how post-modernism witnesses the dismantling of overarching world-views such as Marxism or the Enlightenment project. Lyotard's broad schema has its uses when applied to Irish society, although I don't want to suggest that it should become a new universal yardstick for everything. To set up post-modernism as the new grand narrative would be to contradict its claim that there are no more univocal and universal theories. That said, I believe it can provoke us into a helpful way of looking at ourselves.

3. Jean-François Lyotard, *The Postmodern Condition: A Report on Knowledge*, trans. Geoff Bennington and Brian Massuni, Minneapolis: University of Minnesota Press, 1984.

In this article I would like to look at the demise of the Catholic narrative, the attendant rise of a more person-centred narrative, and the surging narrative of the Celtic Tiger. Then I would like to ask whether these different narratives could somehow intersect. Could the smaller stories of our personal experience and the exciting tale of the Celtic Tiger reconnect with the age-old Christian story? The example I will take to explore this question is sex – so please do read on!

Some people believe that Christianity has nothing to offer Irish people today. I agree with them to the extent that the Christianity they have been presented with has been a travesty of the Good News. However, for all that I have not lost faith. I believe that a revised and renewed Christianity has a wisdom to offer Irish people who are struggling to discover themselves and come to terms with life at the dawn of a new millennium.

The collapse of a big story

Christianity as many experience it in Ireland is a grandiose narrative that clings to power and resists change. And so its prophetic edge has become blunted. The innate capacity of the Christian story to shock, provoke, seduce and inspire has often been replaced by an effort to suppress the niggling realities that challenge orthodoxy to re-examine itself and its presuppositions. And so this inflated narrative has become more and more divorced from the particularity of people's lives despite its claim to retain a universal applicability.

The all-encompassing story or meta-narrative of Catholicism once functioned as the arbiter and judge of the so-called lesser stories in Ireland. It was the only show in town. It operated according to the criteria of inclusion and exclusion, stifling and silencing particular truths and privileging instead truths which claimed the universality of Catholic doctrine. It seems to me that one of the primary reasons for Lyotard's dislike of grand narratives is the fact that they hide and often subjugate the little stories. The fundamental content of our faith – the Good News that Jesus Christ is the Son of God and our Saviour – may constitute such an unlikeable narrative if we see it as the final word about Christianity, the synthesis that negates the value of all the myriad threads in the Bible.

Fortunately, it is not the last word. It is more a gathering point that tries to express the truth of the many different voices and stories in the four Gospels of the New Testament. These Gospels, written more than forty years after Jesus' death, contain several different narratives. Firstly, Jesus' words and deeds. Secondly, the whole oral tradition of the early Church. And, thirdly, the editorial bias of the evangelists which privileged certain stories and excluded others.

If each Gospel narrative is in turn made up of all these layers, it is evident that we can never arrive at a satisfying portrait of Jesus. When we do try to get to know him better he turns out to be an elusive character: on the one hand he does not fit comfortably into bourgeois Christianity – he fraternised with the marginalised and criticised the religious authorities of his time. On the other hand he was no revolutionary – he was surprisingly taciturn about the most controversial political and social questions of his time.

Christian faith emerges from a profusion of small stories. If it suppresses these stories and replaces them with some timeless and mythical Christ, Christianity itself will be impoverished as a result. So we need to see the source of Christianity not as some vacuum-sealed dogma untarnished by history but as an interlocking and often conflicting series of stories. A Christianity that fails to see its debt to these little stories easily becomes a totalising and oppressive doctrine. But as well as doing justice to the stories that surge at its origin, Christianity needs to listen to the stories that surge in the hearts of people today. If faith blocks the smaller stories of contemporary people's lives from expression, it betrays its origins in another way by becoming Bad News. It is most true to itself when it enables the diversity and multiplicity of each of our small stories to surface. Even at the cost of conflict.

Irish Catholics see Irish Catholicism as a Grand Narrative, an often oppressive story. Of course it still has its liberating moments but they have not been the tales we have heard recently. Instead the grand narrative of Irish Catholicism has begun to be deconstructed into some of the negative stories which make it up: sex abuse, Reformation-style stances on ecumenical issues, etc. Meanwhile little liberating narratives have been circulating on the margins: for instance, about lay-people and women and their place in the Church. Our Catholic meta-narrative has been unable to assimilate these new stories into its orthodox construction of reality. Lay Catholics who remain Catholics have responded by creating their own narratives: à la carte Catholicism as it is often disparagingly referred to.

The emergence of small stories
With the demise of the grand Catholic narrative, people are also turning to personal narratives, exploring their own stories. They are sifting through the spectres of the past, unearthing the painful memories and reliving the rawness of hurt in the hope that in the tangled web of this brokenness they might find tentative bricks with which to build a freer and more authentic future. There have been a number of

outstanding personal stories published in the last few years: from Nuala O'Faoláin, Frank McCourt and Seamus Deane, for example. The most significant story is no longer the Catholic story, which seems chained to the past and closed to the future. Organised religion no longer tells us who we are, it only offers facile or unconvincing answers to complex questions. It depresses us by telling us who we thought we were for too long. Instead of looking for the God of dogma, the omniscient and powerful one, storytellers rummage through the ruins of memory and emerge with a little God, so dusty and stained that they often do not recognise it as sacred, so precarious that they sometimes wonder whether it is too fragile a foundation upon which to reconstruct their lives. 'Worse than the ordinary miserable childhood is the miserable Irish childhood, and worse yet is the miserable Irish Catholic childhood.' So writes Frank McCourt on the opening page of *Angela's Ashes*. Four hundred pages later we feel redeemed despite the bleakness and poverty because of a modest and undogmatic God, a bard of humour and vision and musicality.

People are thirsting for an experiential, intelligent and contemporary Catholicism, an adult faith for people who have grown up. The three qualities of experience, intelligence and contemporaneity are all crucial. They do not want a language that attains scholarly respectability at the price of experiential relevance, that orders everything in neat categories and fails to take cognisance of the messiness of real life. They do not want a faith that seeks an intelligence which belongs to a pre-modern age, one that would have suited people who believed the earth was flat but one patently out of touch with people for whom even Einstein is becoming a distant memory.

The voices that speak most compellingly of a new kind of

faith hail from musical and poetic worlds that delve into a primeval layer of our Irishness and our humanity. John O'Donohue's bestseller *Anam Chara* does not discuss the magisterium or Sunday Mass or sex before marriage or popes or canon law. It explores a more catholic and pluriform world – Celtic, Jewish, Buddhist, psychological, artistic. There is something post-modern in this rejection of a monolithic and uniform voice and the re-emergence instead of primordial murmurings which were once consigned to silence. The voices of local, folk, rural and mythological tradition, which were once dismissed in our quest to be modern, have been resurrected into discourse by O'Donohue and others. Ultimately, *Anam Chara* highlights the sacredness of each one's personal story, all those fascinating singular stories that were relegated to insignificance when the Catholic meta-narrative ruled over Irish political and intellectual life. The book has given a powerful kickstart to a new narrative on that we are tentatively engaged: the search for the religious structure in our experience. It is a journey to find and believe in the goodness of our lives, without necessarily subscribing to a body of dogmatic truths.

As their musical career has developed, U2 has tried to retain a transcendence minus the God of orthodoxy. They have attempted to explore the texture of a new sense of God in their songs, unapologetically borrowing insights from different stories – religious and secular – and bringing them together in their unique way. When they launched their most recent album, *Pop,* in February 1997, Bono replied to a question from a French journalist by saying, 'We still have the same ideals, we've just learnt to look like we don't.'

They have given a glitzy wrapping to their serious aspirations. Their world tour, Pop Mart, which kicked off in

Las Vegas, **was an extravagant** spectacle with garish overblown **props that** represented a tongue-in-cheek celebration **of pop culture.** Yet their fascination with God managed to **seep through, as** did their sensitivity to his felt absence by **so many people.** In the song from *Pop* called 'Wake Up Dead Man', **which** was originally intended for the album *Zooropa*, Bono wails at God as a modern psalmist might, 'Jesus help me/I'm all alone in this world.... Tell me the story/The one about Eternity/And the way it's gonna be'.

There are occasional moments of confusion in the new narrative of Irish Catholicism, when the plot seems to turn back on itself, when we raid the memory banks of nostalgia and an album such as *Faith of Our Fathers* becomes a phenomenal hit. But it is a gesture that expresses the sadness of an inevitable farewell, not the desire to reconstruct a meaning system that has passed its sell-by date.

On the whole we prefer a selective amnesia about our history. The *Riverdance* show is a striking instance of this vast forgetfulness. It was an Australian friend who pointed out to me that in telling the Irish story from its Celtic roots to its flowering in the diaspora, the show's only reference to Christianity was a small church in one of Robert Ballagh's brilliant design projections. In other words, the show depicts the river of Celtic culture gushing from a pre-Christian past into a post-Christian future. The unspoken implication is that the Catholic thing was a polluted tributary leading nowhere.

The new narratives we are fashioning in Ireland are not altogether unlike that of the nineteen-year-old Joyce:

> He was no longer a Christian himself; but he converted the temple to new uses instead of trying to knock it down, regarding it as a superior kind of human folly and

one which, interpreted by a secular artist, contained obscure bits of truth.[4]

As a young man Joyce was fed up with the spiritual paralysis of Irish Catholicism. He was angry at the cringing dependence it encouraged in his compatriots. He was revolted by the moral stranglehold it held over them. Of course this stance represented a portrait of this artist as *a young man*. His stance evolved throughout his life. His perspective evolved beyond that of an angry youth. Perhaps we are at a similar point to the young Joyce. We need to recognise our anger at the Church and listen to the hurt we feel. Out of this we may be able to bring forth something new, retaining what is good and leaving aside what is harmful.

For the moment, though, many people have had enough. They need to be liberated from organised religion for a while. It is not helping them to forge a new sense of who they can be in the smithy of their souls. It speaks an official and bureaucratic language that constitutes abysmal prose: 'words, words, words', as Hamlet put it. What they are looking for is poetry.

The Church does not offer the opportunity for people to weave a definite pattern out of the confused tangle of their lives. They need a space in which to tell the untold story of their lives. If we cannot name and tell our story, life becomes passive endurance. We tell stories in order to make what is hidden and confused intelligible for ourselves as well as for others. We also tell stories in order that the darkness such tales usher into the light will not become obscure again.

---

4.   Richard Ellman, *James Joyce*, New York: Oxford University Press, 1982, p.66.

'There are… victims whose suffering cries less for vengeance than for narration' (Paul Ricoeur). In telling our stories we not only describe our experience, we prioritise it, we identify what is good and bad, thereby envisioning what we want and do not want for the future. Telling our stories restores meaning and gives direction to life.

I recently watched Neil Jordan's film of Patrick McCabe's novel, *The Butcher Boy*. It seemed to me that McCabe was telling a story that few of us have the courage to face right now. A small story, the story of a child, yet explosive in its impact, like the continual allusions in the film to the possibility of an atomic war. It is the story of twelve-year-old Francie Brady in early sixties Ireland. He kills his neighbour Mrs Nugent with an abattoir bolt-gun and then hacks up her body. McCabe does not suggest that the boy is a little monster. Neither does he blame the boy's environment for this savage act. And this despite the terribly raw deal Francie gets from life – Mrs Nugent calls his family 'pigs', his mother kills herself, a priest abuses him, his father dies. But McCabe does not depict him as a victim. He walks a tightrope, suggesting that this ordinary child is also a psychopath, that the innocence of childhood is mixed up with awful cruelty.

The opening song of the film set me thinking. 'Mack the Knife' was written by Bertolt Brecht and Kurt Weill, and formed part of *The Threepenny Opera*, their show which was so popular in the cabaret circuit of the Weimar Republic, the period immediately preceding the explosion of the mayhem and brutality of Nazism. Brecht was familiar with a story from Nietzsche's *Thus Spoke Zarathustra* about a crazed murderer who was fixated on 'the joy of the knife'. There is something Nietzschean about this film and not only in Francie's evident joy in dismembering Mrs Nugent. There is also the nihilism expressed by the abyss of violence which opens up – visually conveyed by the atomic mushroom cloud that rises from a lake or by the wasp-headed clergyman on horseback in a burning and desolate landscape. And there are many other rumblings of Nietzsche: Francie versus the herd mentality of those around him, Francie creating his own morality, the sense that God might be dead although people get excited about sightings of the Virgin Mary. Most of all Nietzsche is present in the skilful way in which Jordan places us inside Francie's head and brings us to the abyss along with him, showing us what a world without God or grammar, without a supernatural or natural order, might look like. Among the many other things this harrowing and excellent film conveyed to me was the confirmation that if the little narratives of our lives are not connected to something larger we are left terribly alone to face the explosive and subterranean power that threatens to burst forth from the depths of ourselves. Nietzsche wanted to face this nihilism: he knew it would either destroy him or make him stronger. Nietzsche went mad. In Jordan's film, Francie is incarcerated in a mental institution from which he is released years later, his chaotic and violent drives drugged into dullness.

The big story of the Celtic Tiger

We Irish are connecting the little stories of our lives to larger tales. Constant talk of the Celtic Tiger is shaping a brash new meta-narrative. It has so dominated the headlines that it has pushed deprivation to the inside pages of our national newspapers. Our new-found affluence may be as much a state of mind as anything else yet this big story has become an interpretative lens with which we see other lesser stories. We talk so much of our booming and buoyant economy that the reality of a third of our children living in poverty seems unworthy of attention, an inevitable cost of change. Because of the power of this new meta-narrative we filter out glaring problems that will not go away. A recent study by Anne Power called *Estates on the Edge* concludes that Irish public housing estates are the most severely stigmatised in Europe. Power sees society as reaching a watershed where old welfare remedies amount to no more than sticking-plaster on the social wounds we face. Meanwhile the cherished narrative of the Celtic Tiger marches on: *The Irish Times* recently inaugurated two substantial business supplements to their Friday edition. The tiger is ready to pounce on the future and dig its claws into the wealth of the coming millennium (though there are tell-tale signs that this narrative is too grandiose and that the much vaunted tiger amounts to no more than an excited cat).

The Celtic Tiger is a seductive sobriquet for today's Ireland. It reminds us of the original Asian Tigers who were catapulted from low levels of development to become overnight economic miracles – and whose economies are now becoming increasingly shaky. The image of a tiger can lead us to think that it was our own strength and power that got us here, whereas we know there was also a felicitous conjuncture of circumstances: an educated English-speaking work force, generous government grants to multinationals, etc. The word 'Celtic' resonates romance, culture, spirituality, a golden age, an ancient and noble lineage…. It dresses up capitalism so well that it almost comes disguised as something quaint and innocuous. Yet in many ways the Celtic Tiger is inimical to a Christian ethos.

In certain ways, however, the Celtic Tiger is about more than money and getting rich. It certainly has a strong element of 'mé-féinism', of a frenzied surge towards success, with all its negative side-effects. Suicide is on the increase in Ireland and the World Health Organisation recently forecast depression as the main cause of disability in the developed world by the year 2020. Nevertheless the Celtic Tiger is also a spiritual appellation which is uniquely suited to the time of transition in which we find ourselves. In a time where everything is changing, only a spiritual term has enough depth to help us understand ourselves. Beyond its economic applicability, the Celtic Tiger says something about how we understand ourselves as strong (tigerlike) in a new way and as once again connected to an enlightened moment of our history (Celtic).

This sense of strength is manifested in many ways. Take our fertility rate. The number of births in the third quarter of 1997, between July and September, was the highest figure for ten years, according to the Central Statistics Office. Or take the fifteen thousand people, many of them in their twenties, who felt empowered to migrate or return to Ireland in the year up until April 1997. This was up from eight thousand in 1995-6 and up from zero in previous years. Take the burgeoning interest in the arts. 350,000 people visited the Irish Museum of Modern Art in 1997, breaking all records. Take our late twentieth-century fascination with discovering our inner power, which embraces an intricate tangle of New Age quests and orthodox thirsts. There is a big interest in psychology, in holistic spiritualities that take the body seriously, in astrology, reflexology, massage, aromatherapy, and in certain devotional practices like the age-old penitential pilgrimage to Lough Derg. The *X-Files* retain immense popularity among a young audience. *The Fortean Times* is a monthly magazine devoted to strange phenomena, portents and prodigies, which you can find in many newsagents. Sky One daily broadcasts programmes linked with the paranormal: Tuesday at 10.00pm it's *The Extraordinary*, Wednesday at 10.00pm *Millennium*, Friday at 8.00pm *Highlander*, Saturday at 8.00pm is *Buffy The Vampire Slayer*, Sunday at 8.00pm *Earth: The Final Conflict*, 9.00pm *The X-Files*, and, of course, *Star Trek* every day of the week.

People are saying yes to spirituality but no to the enterprises that have inadequately incarnated it in institutional form. The supernatural has retreated from the public sphere and become a private interest. It is part of a millennial introspectiveness. This is in danger of leaving us with an emasculated faith, one that is aware of individuals on the margins of society, but which fails to put our marginalising society itself under the spotlight. Such a faith suits capitalism because it no longer threatens it. Although many people help out in community service and programmes for the underprivileged, they do not think of tackling the bigger structural issues which lead to poverty and exclusion. Even post-modernists would recognise that the collapse of meta-narratives such as Christianity and Marxism has lessened our lives. These systems achieved much good, including the great impetus they gave to the endeavour to transform society as well as the attempt to answer more immediate needs.

The Celtic Tiger is not a simple story, however. It is not a matter of a ferocious beast of prey casually tossing everything else aside. The reality is more complex and multifaceted. The ambiguous relationship between the economic Celtic Tiger and the emerging strength of a new spiritual voice in the midst of this Tiger was captured for me by an edition of the

Late Late Show (the longest-running live chat show ever – some narrative!) from January 1998.

Gay Byrne started with a interview of Lorraine Keane. I warmed to this attractive, ambitious and articulate young woman, whose voice is so familiar over the radio waves from the AA Roadwatch. Then she was asked to stay while three environmental protesters from the Glen of the Downs came on. As they spoke with religious fervour and evangelical joy, she suddenly came across as less sympathetic.

If I were to sketch the contrasts that struck me, it would look something like this:

Lorraine Keane	Eco-Warriors
Technology (AA, roads)	Ecology (trees, nature)
Individualistic	Communitarian
Ambitious mapping of career	Eco-vocation as primary
Artificial accent	Voice of nature
Svelte, sophisticated, synthetic clothing	Natural knits, woollens
Wanting an antique car	Happy in a tree-house
Belief in affluence	Sceptical about consumerism

This clash of values is symptomatic of Ireland in 1998: a society excited by affluence yet with an enduring and questioning spirituality articulated in a new way by the eco-warriors. Paradoxically they appeared at first as marginal and eccentric figures. Lorraine Keane occupied the centre of normality. As Gay Byrne and the audience began to see more and more evidence of the focused and happy human beings behind the scruffy exteriors, the eco-activists appeared to epitomise true sanity. They did not fit the stereotype of ineffective romantics who sponge off society. They were not poor. They were not spongers. They were educated, intelligent and at home with advanced technology (one of them worked in the multi-media business).

It also struck me that twenty years ago these three young people with glowing expressions and burning enthusiasm might have been candidates for the priesthood and religious life. I tried to imagine how priests, nuns and brothers would appear if they were sitting in a panel alongside these eco-warriors today. I came up with the following mischievous contrasts:

Eco-warriors	**Catholic clergy and religious**
happy and young	depressed and elderly
creative and experimental	unimaginative and cautious
exotic and marginal	boring and mainstream
confident and audacious	perplexed and apologetic
strong sense of identity	self-questioning
egalitarian	hierarchical
recovering a golden past	chained to a burdensome past

Uniting the stories with the help of sex

I now want to take all this forward. I will try to show how the exciting story of the Celtic Tiger, our own personal stories, and the Good News can creatively come together. I want to demonstrate how this can occur through taking an uncensored view of the sex-life of God! Before I do that I want to stress that the time is ripe for bringing God and sex together. Sex has become a more open and discussed topic in the personal lives of Irish people as well as at a wider social level. Dublin was recently rated as one of the top party towns in Europe and our buoyant economy has produced a rising fertility rate. However, the Celtic Tiger can repress the sexual drive in less obvious ways: our concern with success and technique can invade sexuality too and lead us to tame the passion of sex by trying to master its mystery with banal how-to-do-it manuals. And the pressure of working in a fast-paced world can leave little energy or space for sex. According to a Mills & Boon survey published on 9 February 1998, 70 per cent of Irish women say they haven't enough time to make love!

What I would like to ask is: can we find anything in the narratives and tales of Christianity to enrich sex and sexuality? I am sure we would all agree that our sexuality needs improvement. Even the Mills & Boon survey I just mentioned suggests as much: almost half of the Irish women surveyed were keen to send their partners off to romance school. Although romance school might seem like a practical idea, many of us would find it more difficult to believe that religion could be of much use to our sexuality. After all, it kept the lid on libido for an awfully long time. But before you make up your mind definitively, just listen to what the pop star Madonna has to say on this heated subject. Speaking to Norman Mailer in an *Esquire* interview of 1994, this daughter of Catholic parents commented:

> I do believe religion and eroticism are absolutely related. And I think my original feelings of sexuality and eroticism originated in going to church.

Although I do not subscribe to her sizzling cocktail of sex and religion, there is more than a grain of truth in what Madonna says. We need to reintegrate sexuality into our Christianity. We have forgotten or concealed the fact that God is more sexual than any of us. This may seem shocking until we reflect that God created us as sexual beings, male and female, and we are created in his image. We hesitate at conceiving of God as a sexual being because our experience of sex and sexuality is ambiguous and narrow. Ambiguous, because sex causes pain as well as pleasure, hurt along with happiness. Narrow, because we tend to reduce sex to genital penetration. We instinctively think that sex is something we do. And so we are shocked at the notion that a priest might have a sexual life, unless we enlarge our idea of sex to think of it as something which is a quality of our being. A priest is a sexual being, a human being of the male sex (at least in the Roman Catholic Church) and everything he does is done as a male. He cannot not be sexual.

God is more sexually liberated than we are. His sexuality is not distorted by egoism or self-seeking. It is a full expression of who God is, whereas the human experience of sexual intercourse, no matter how wonderful, can never fully express the selves of the lovers. There is always more of us to be discovered, expressed and communicated. God's sexuality is at a higher level than ours. It is perfectly integrated into his nature. However, we do not know in what way God expresses his sexuality. We can only surmise that the joy and passion we experience in human sexual love are merely a shadow of his.

We can enlarge and ennoble our notion of sexuality if we apply it to the mystery of the love life within God, the ecstatic self-giving that occurs between Father, Son and Spirit. For a long time we Irish have followed St Patrick's example in grasping at the shamrock to help us picture the Trinity. That is okay for children. But for over-eighteens, sexual love would be a much more real (and graphic!) analogy. Not that it will explain the mystery of the Trinity, for in that case the Trinity would cease to be a mystery. But it can help us to identify its contours more clearly.

In the sexual union of a man and woman, there is such physical intimacy that there is no longer any distance between the two. And yet, despite there being no space between them, a third person, a child, emerges. He materialises where there had been no space. This third person is not a stranger. The child, after all, is the fruit of their love. At the same time the child is not simply the sum of the two lovers. He is much more. He is another person. On the one hand, the child's existence is evidence of their love. On the other hand, his life is also the proof that their love reaches beyond themselves. True love is creative. The lovers go further than themselves and bring forth life.

God is love. Pure love means that one is purely for the other, that the other always has priority. The Father gives himself fully to the Son. He surrenders himself. The Son receives the self of the Father. He receives everything that he is from the Father. And all he desires in return is to reciprocate this love and give himself fully back to the Father. The unexpected result of this mutual surrender of love is a third person, the Spirit. The Spirit is the fruit of the love between the Father and Son. Of course he is more than the fruit; he is also a person in his own right. The Spirit, like the Father and Son, is a being of love. All he desires is to be the perfect expression of the love between the Father and the Son.

The model of human sexual love helps us to make some sense, however inadequate, of the Trinity. And it helps ennoble our understanding of sex. It challenges the idea that sex is something dirty. It also challenges the illusion that sex is purely material, since we can use the analogy of sex to think about God who is essentially spirit. In fact, sex is not merely a matter of the body, even though people have sex with one another in and through their bodies. But when someone says,

'I have sex twice a week', the 'I' to which they are referring is more than the body. Otherwise they could simply have left it at 'My body has sex twice a week'.

God is not bodily as we are. God is spirit. So in comparing human sexual love to the love in the Trinity we have to remember that the physical union between a man and woman is not the centre of this analogy. What is central in the analogy is what this physical union expresses. The physical union between lovers ideally expresses their total and self-surrendering love, i.e. something spiritual. Of course it is rarely the physical union that is of sole importance in sex either. The joy we feel in sex is bodily but also very much linked to a particular person who is more than a body. There is a fine example of this in the Jewish Bible. In the twenty-ninth chapter of Genesis, Jacob has sex with Leah, mistakenly assuming her to be Rachel, because her face is veiled. Jacob only realises he has been duped the next day. He thoroughly enjoys the night spent with Leah because he thinks he is with Rachel, the woman of his desires.

Even though sex is more spiritual in God, this does not make it less pleasurable. On the contrary, because God is the source of sex, it is natural to expect sex to be part of who God is in a much richer way than it is part of who we are. For God, sex is not a matter of two bodies intertwining for a brief period of intense joy. It is a matter of spirits and personalities totally interpenetrating in an eternal explosion of ecstasy. If we were to transpose the love life of the Trinity into human terms, it would be like being in the continual passionate embrace of the one you love most while simultaneously delighting in the arrival of one's perfect newborn child.

But of course we cannot readily translate the love life of God into our terms because God is beyond time. So there is no period of pregnancy, no time lapse before the arrival of the Spirit. All is instantaneous in God. There is no waiting. There is no gap between desire and fulfilment. It happens once. This once is now. And so this once is always. In other words, this mutual self-surrender is continually happening within the community we call God. The Father is continually surrendering himself fully to the Son. The Son is continually receiving and returning this infinite love. And the Spirit is continually springing forth as the expression of their mutual surrender.

Taking the analogy of human sexual love as a way of better appreciating the mystery of the Trinity might seem more than novel. It might come across as provocative and downright disrespectful. That is because we have inherited a mistrust of the body and of sex. Therefore, talking about the Trinity in sexual terms seems to demean the greatness of God by implicating him in baseness. The reverse is true. If we could not talk of the Trinity in sexual terms, then we would be irremediably base, because we would be unable to find any traces of God in our human experience of sexuality. That would also mean we could not genuinely exalt him because he would be excluded from one of the deepest drives and powers inside of us: sex.

Conclusion

I have looked at the decline of the Grand Narrative of Irish Catholicism and the rise of the Celtic Tiger as well as the emergence of personal quests for meaning. I have been foolhardy enough to take the provocative example of sex, a classic twentieth-century obsession, in order to see whether the stories that preoccupy ordinary people can be integrated into the Good News, in a manner that deepens these stories and makes Christianity more real. To sum up, I believe that we need to re-imagine the traditional ways we conceive of God and religion. We need to allow new narratives to be told about the sacred. I have suggested in this article that we can take the narratives of our own lives and of our own society as starting points. Admittedly they are imperfect points of departure. The emerging narratives of the new Ireland are still in chrysalis. Yet God's voice speaks elusively within them, not with the fullness of presence but with the promise of hope. It requires effort and imagination to carry out the double task of identifying God's imprint in the texts of our lives and of linking our personal stories and the story of the new Ireland with the stories that form the Good News of Christianity. Thankfully we Irish have never lacked imagination.

OUTPOURINGS OF A SPIRITUAL PYGMY

Breda O'Brien

Shortly before Easter, it emerged that three girls in the fifth-year religion class I teach were certain that they had never heard of Judas. Such moments are sent to keep teachers humble. This was more, however, than a geography teacher discovering that three of her class profess ignorance of the existence of the Shannon. It summed up the change in culture which has happened with astonishing speed in Ireland. It confirmed that unless you are in daily contact with young people, you are unlikely to be aware of the greatest generation gap in Irish history.

On one side of the divide is a generation who either believed as a matter of course or who passionately wrestled with aspects of faith and morals that outraged them. On the other side is a generation of young Irish people who are mostly benignly tolerant of anyone's individual choice to believe, but who are astonished to think that it should or could be more than a personal lifestyle choice. It is summed up in their 'whatever you are into' approach to life. Be a Christian or a vegetarian or a Rastafarian so long as you are not boring about it. They are faintly embarrassed on behalf of anyone who thinks that a particular faith has a claim to universality or any validity beyond what an individual gives to it.

A philosopher might call it post-modernism. It has been discussed at length by writers such as Michael Paul Gallagher.[1] It is the greatest challenge facing those who believe that the gospel of Jesus Christ is more than a 'whatever you are having yourself' choice.

John Waters, in his provocative book *An Intelligent Person's Guide to Modern Ireland,* selects 1960 as the moment of the birth of modern Ireland.[2] It is, of course, partly a tongue-in-cheek choice, because it is so absolutely arbitrary as a moment. For my purposes I think 1980 is probably as good a standpoint as any from which to start an examination of a huge cultural change, if only because anyone now in second-level education was born after that date. More significantly, their parents are members of a cusp generation – those who experienced the Catholic Church before and after Vatican Two.

In 1980 the Pope had just been to Ireland and the visit had been hugely successful. Fr Michael Cleary and Bishop Eamon Casey were prominent in the celebrations. There was an air of excitement and revitalisation around, particularly in relation to initiatives with young people. If anyone had predicted that within fifteen years the word most young people would associate with 'priest' was paedophile, they would have been laughed at.

The expected blossoming of the Irish Catholic Church did not happen. Some worthwhile initiatives began and are still in existence, but the questioning of the Church by young people

1. See Chapter Eight, 'Postmodernism – Friend or Foe' in *Clashing Symbols – An Introduction to Faith And Culture*, Michael Paul Gallagher SJ, London: Darton, Longman and Todd, 1997.
2. Chapter 2, 'The Moment of Rupture', London: Duckworth and Co., 1997.

in the eighties had given way within a decade to something infinitely worse than hostility. It was almost as if a particular way of expressing faith was so irrelevant to their lives that it was not worth even arguing about.

This was probably more true in urban than in rural areas, but for the most part faith moved from the public arena to the private during this time.

Many young adults would describe themselves as spiritual, but generally theirs is an intensely personal spirituality, a comfort zone in a sometimes chaotic world. It is not open to a wider tradition which would challenge some of its more self-centred manifestations. It is certainly not the expression of a communal identity, nor does it usually have a strong social conscience.

So what happened? To these young people Vatican Two is an event in pre-history, because it happened years before they were born. The kind of Church they grew up in was heavily into social justice, both here and overseas. This is one aspect that has rubbed off, because young people will cheerfully push beds or fast for the developing world. They are less likely to want to change any aspect of their often comfortable lifestyles if it is pointed out that their comparative wealth sustains inequality in two-thirds of the world. That is a bridge too far.

Probably the most important feature of the Church they grew up in is that it was just a voice among other voices. It was not the dominant feature of the landscape.

It is customary to blame the influence of the media for the erosion in the importance of the Church. This is a simplistic approach, but the grain of truth within its over-simplification deserves to be explored.

Media practitioners in Ireland like to think of themselves as an iconoclastic lot. In fact, they are alarmingly similar in their views. Urban-minded if not living in urban areas, middle-class, anti-clerical, what is described as liberal on social issues – boringly predictable, in fact. John Healy, John Waters and Desmond Fennell[3] have done a far better job than I could on their characteristics, so I won't linger on it.

But some years ago I was intrigued to learn that the director of a very influential media organisation had conducted Myers Briggs personality tests on the personnel who worked for it. An inordinately large number of them fell into what is termed the ENFP category ('Extrovert, Intuitive, Feeling, Perceptive'). The fascinating thing about this is that the ENFPs are conservers of tradition – not iconoclasts. The only reason that media people are not seen as the innate conservatives that they actually are, is that they are conserving a tradition of mild anti-authority and anti-institutionalism.

The living network of faith which sustains many people, whether it be through Mass-going, involvement in work for justice or in parish organisations, is outside the experience of many journalists and therefore goes unreported.

The lack of diversity of voices in the media has meant that our young people have grown up with something in the ether which whispers and sometimes bellows that the Church is a bastion of repression and outdated oppressive values. They have grown up with a new 'tradition', a conventional wisdom that is not open to question any more than the goodness of the Church was once open to question.

In short, they are carrying the baggage of their elders, most of whom do not have a clue what the current reality of the

3. See Chapter 10, 'Getting to Know Dublin 4' in *Heresy –The Battle of Ideas In Modern Ireland,* Desmond Fennell, Belfast: Blackstaff Press, 1993.

Church is. They are stunned by facts such as the attendances at novenas. Nobody else is, but they are. This negative baggage has been passed on to a younger generation who have never experienced anything remotely approaching oppression from their Church.

Of course, it is questionable how oppressed these media people were in the first place. A future generation might query the smug self-satisfaction of today, where we seem to accept that a significant portion of our tiny population is inevitably condemned to poverty. A future generation might wonder where the iconoclasts were while this was happening, and find, surprisingly enough, that they were in the Church, not the media.

It is astonishing but true that in this country, if you wish to find truly radical solutions to the inbuilt injustices in our system, you do not look to the parties of the Left, or even to the once-vaunted social consciences of the larger parties. You look to the Church. You look to Brigid Reynolds and Seán Healy of CORI,[4] to Stanislaus Kennedy and Peter McVerry.[5]

The Church herself is far from blameless. I have to admit that I cringe when I hear anyone talking about the 'spirit of Vatican Two'. Usually it means what the speaker wished Vatican Two had said or done, rather than what the documents actually contain. The documents are often prophetic, challenging and a source of inspiration. Yet looking back on it as a phenomenon some thirty-five years later, some very strange things were done in the name of Vatican Two.

I have a memory from childhood of my mother being

---

4. *Social Policy In Ireland – Principles, Practices and Problems,* ed. Sean Healy and Brigid Reynolds, Dublin: Oak Tree Press, 1998.
5. Cf. 'A Personal Journey' and 'Moments of Grace' in *Spiritual Journeys,* ed. Stanislaus Kennedy, Dublin: Veritas, 1997.

upset because the lovely marble altar to Our Lady in our little village church had been demolished with sledgehammers in the name of reform. A lot of sledgehammers were gleefully taken out, and much of what was demolished was both beautiful and valuable.

That includes education in basic tenets of the Catholic faith. A lot of young people today receive their first exposure to the concept of transubstantiation in a Junior Cert history class on the Reformation. It is not considered too difficult or obscure a concept there. Why does the religion class shy away from such ideas which are central to Catholic belief?

Marshall McLuhan was writing in the 1960s of a generation who were more visually than print oriented, who were 'hot' rather than 'cold', for whom emotion was more important than intellect. At precisely the same moment, the Church was stripping from its liturgy much that was visually and sensually appealing and replacing it with something much more cerebral. Out with the incense and candles, processions, flowers, statues. Out with much that was emotionally sustaining and that fed the soul. We could learn a great deal from our Eastern Orthodox brethren with regard to the use of icons, candles, darkness and singing.

Some of the churches built at that time have all the atmosphere of an aircraft hangar. Because churches were supposed to be places where the community came to celebrate together, not places of private devotion, a kind of stripped-down minimalism came into vogue.

How a church looks may seem a minor detail, but we are not disembodied spirits. We need places that nourish and calm us, and that allow the divine to enter our fractured, frantic souls. In recent times there has been a return to the creation of spaces that feed our souls. The beautiful new church in Naas, which is rich with symbolism, is an example.

Yet it still has to be said that the Church dispensed with much that was feminine, maternal and nourishing, at a time when she was supposed to be paying much more attention to the role of women.

Someone gave me Margaret Hebblethwaite's *Motherhood and God* after the birth of my first child. At the time it was first published in 1984 it was mildly controversial because of the author's exploration of feminine images of God. Far from being controversial it is a mining of a rich seam of biblical, patristic and theological imagery of God, which means a great deal to me as a woman and a mother.

Much of the discussion of the role of women in the Church has centred around what for me is an utterly sterile issue – that of the ordination of women. Outside of élite theological circles, I have never met a woman remotely bothered about it. But I have met very many women bothered by how best to bring up families in a rapidly changing world, how to share a faith with a generation which has grown up in a completely different context.

Margaret Hebblethwaite's book describes the frustrations, the heights and the depths of family life. I was touched and affectionately amused that the prayer she choose to say during labour was the 'Our Father'.[6] (Remember, this is a book dedicated to exploring feminine images of God!) Having read this book, I decided I would pray the Prayer to the Guardian Angel during contractions in my second labour. Yes, that simple prayer people over thirty learnt as children. I know

---

6. Chapter 12, 'The Third Birth', p. 79, *Motherhood And God,* Margaret Hebblethwaite, London: Geoffrey Chapman, 1984.

admitting this consigns me to the ranks of the feebleminded, so I may as well concede that I attend Mass and light candles as well. Anyway, praying that way helped to make a quite long and painful labour one of the most beautiful experiences of my life, one that fills me with quiet joy every time I think of it.

There are not too many books of theology where the agony and joy of birth leads into a meditation on the nature of God. The Church has a rich theology on family, but the practice falls down somewhat. As an idealistic teenager I was told by a well-known priest who gave retreats that I should become a nun, because the best way to serve God was as a priest, the second as a nun. He did not give me a third option.

I wish I could claim that I was scarred for life by this experience but fortunately I wasn't. Even at that age I was contrary enough to know that he was simply wrong. I had no vocation to a religious order then or later.

There are many movements within the Church which emphasise family and they are very worthwhile. Yet, as Noreen O'Carroll says in her recent book *Virginia's Questions*, there are many people who are not designed to be members of movements, who are not 'clubbable'.[7]

The broad Church needs to be really aware, supportive and challenging of families. While acknowledging that it is within families that most of us live our vocation, we also need to be continually challenged to be aware of and contributing to the world outside our own family.

Much of what is written about families is very idealistic, and seems not to have come from people who have ever

---

7. Chapter 11, 'Religious Groups', p. 121 in *Virginia's Questions – Why I am Still A Catholic,* Noreen O'Carroll, Dublin: Columba Press, 1998.

experienced the incandescent rage which a stubborn toddler can ignite in you.

This kind of comment usually leads straight on to a demand for an end to celibacy so that our ministers will be more understanding of mundane family life. I have to say that I find that the most inane response possible, and that it makes as much sense as advocating celibacy for married couples.

I hope that is not hurtful for the priests for whom celibacy is difficult and painful. All I am saying is that ordained ministry is for a minority of Catholics. Marriage and family are still the norm for most. This does not render other forms of family or single life second class, but in our correct sensitivity to those other forms we should not forget that the majority also need consideration and help.

The Church is often overly clerical in its outlook, and those lay people who become involved on a professional level through, for example, taking degrees in theology, often become sucked into that. Clerical politics centres around debates about who should be appointed bishop, where and by what method, or how lay people can get more power in the church, as if power were a central issue.

Jesus gave the answer to all of that when the ambitious mother came to plead for positions for her sons at his right and left side. He told her bluntly that if they could face the suffering which he would face they could have any position they liked. In other words, seeking more power is entirely the wrong approach. The Church should not be a political party with one faction continually jockeying for control at the expense of another. The gospel is supposed to be about seeking the ability to serve, to be the least of the brethren (cf. Matthew 20:20-28).

The divisions in the Church are, in themselves, a source of scandal. You have the sorry spectacle of the committed arguing about theological niceties while young people are ignorant of the names of the four evangelists.

Particularly damaging is the suspicion with which the 'liberal' wing of the Church regards the 'conservative' wing and vice versa. We have no business importing ideological divisions into the Church. The Church really is a treasure house, but most people are selective about which bits they want. For example, why is it that those who are most prophetic in the Church because of their commitment to the poor and dispossessed are often unwilling to see abortion as anything other than an issue of personal morality? Some of the people who have done most to challenge the excessive individualism of our society cannot go the extra mile to see that abortion advocacy is springing from exactly the same ideological well. Unfortunately, this means they intensify the loneliness of the decisions which thousands of Irish women face, because by removing the community dimension they also remove community responsibility.

Equally, why do those who see clearly the issues involved in abortion often prefer to ignore or sideline the Church's teaching on poverty and social solidarity from *Rerum novarum* onward? Catholic morality should be a seamless garment – respect for life and the conditions in which people have to live it from womb to tomb. Surely those who ignore the Church's clear teaching on this are as 'à la carte' as those who ignore the Church's teaching on sexual morality?

Finally, when I was asked to contribute to this book, I mentally titled my own contribution 'The Outpourings of a Spiritual Pygmy'. I then realised that this would be seen as a woeful and regrettable lack of self-esteem on my part, instead of a wry and absolutely accurate assessment of my spiritual condition. For someone with the background and advantages that I have, my spiritual development is pitiful. I do not need my self-esteem massaged. I need to be challenged to tackle that pathetic state of affairs.

Where the Church has become a purveyor of pop psychology, more into empowerment and the Enneagram than into evangelisation, it has become a travesty of itself. As far as I know, Jesus never inquired into anyone's self-esteem, but just asked them to take up their cross daily and follow him. That is why his words echo across the centuries, as fresh and radical today as the day they were spoken.

More than most I have reason to be grateful to a Church that has shaped and fed me. It is full of good people, lay and ordained, who try to live their lives, with the help of the grace of God, to bring about a better world.

The Catholic Church in Ireland has had a crisis from which it is slowly recovering. It is less a temporal power as a result, and that I believe is good. The Church should always be more of a voice crying in the wilderness and less of a seat at the table of privilege. That's the way Jesus is, anyway.

THE FRONTIER OF THE WORD

Anthony Draper

The writer of secular fiction

The relationship between the artist and the Church is a vast and complex one. For centuries the Church was one of the great patrons of the arts. Religious stories and characters provided the dominant themes for the sculptor, painter, poet and playwright. The motivation too was also professedly religious. The Church still commissions works of art, some artists deal with religious themes and some state an explicit religious motivation. However, that direct relationship between Church and art, while important, is not the central one at the present time and so the more relevant question now is to investigate the relationship between the secular artist and the Church. This paper does not aim to investigate such a vast question, but simply to concentrate on one type of artist, namely the writer of serious fiction, and to offer a personal reflection on the richness that serious fiction offers to the Church and the theologian. The focus is on the serious writer of secular fiction, that is, the writer not avowedly religious and not dealing explicitly with religious themes, who is serious not in the sense of glum or ponderous, but serious as opposed to trivial. What such an artist has to say may not be a direct address to the Church or theology, but can be heard by paying attention to the themes chosen, the insights offered and in the very approach the writer takes in creating the work of art. The remarks offered here arise from a deep conviction that neither the Church nor theology are giving sufficient attention to the creative writer and by doing so both could speak more appropriately to the world today.

The artist is independent

From the outset one fact must remain sharply in focus in any musing on this complex area. The writer, indeed every artist, must speak in a way true to his or her own integrity. The work of art must always be critiqued in terms of artistic quality, and stands or falls on that criterion. The writer must be free to be faithful to his or her artistic vision. Whether that vision pleases or displeases the Church, or whether the work offers a significant contribution to theological discourse is another matter. The creative writer is not the servant of the Church or the theologian, and at times the greater contribution to theology may be made precisely where the artistic vision is at odds with the theologian's.

Sacred or secular?

The loss of a specific religious motivation and subject matter must not be unduly lamented. The rigid separation in the past between sacred and secular, between the holy and the profane is much more subtly understood in recent decades. Traditionally, theology seemed to suggest that one moved from a secular reality, where God was not thought to be present, into a sacred space where a real meeting with God was possible. Having had this encounter in the sacred place one returned again to the secular pursuits of this profane 'godless' world. This division of human experience into compartments was too simple. Theologians now stress that no domain of human activity is removed from the action of

God's loving presence, and seeking an experience of the sacred is still valid, not as a temporary escape from the profane, but as a way of evoking and deepening an appreciation of the sacredness of all reality. This description, so central to sacramental theology, is illuminating when applied to the world of serious fiction. The writer who does not choose religious themes or work out of an explicitly religious motivation cannot be categorised in such a fashion as to convey the impression that the work is 'merely secular' and therefore separated from God. The reality of human life is, in the Christian perspective, the world of God's creation, loved and redeemed by Jesus Christ and filled with the Spirit on its way to an eternal destiny. Therefore, the serious writer, whether believer or not, whose work strives to see into the depth of human experience, or one particle of it, is providing rich fare for the theologian. 'God is in the bits and pieces of every day', wrote Patrick Kavanagh, and the one who sheds light on those bits and pieces must surely be involved in revelation. Wendy Beckett observes that all great art is spiritual, but this does not involve religious ichnography or religious imagery. On the contrary 'the impact may be all the greater for being anonymous and pure'.[1] She then adds, with even more precision, that 'non-religious forms of spiritual art can be more immediately effective than the work in which dogmatism or narrative may be used to direct the impact'.[2] It would therefore be depressingly facile if the Church were to dismiss an author as merely secular (in the old sense), and thereby avoid paying attention to a view of reality that cries out for some theological reflection.

---

1. Wendy Beckett, *Art and the Sacred,* London: Random Century, 1992, p. 9.
2. Ibid.

The artistic canvas

Art is founded on the assumption that all of human life is open for exploration and reflection. No dimension may be kept from view. Every imaginable relationship, state, situation and emotion provides material for the artist. It is a vast panorama. Out of this enormous spectrum, the artist concentrates on one particular portion. This may be a tiny particle in the case of the poem or short story; a broader agenda for drama, and a wider spectrum again in the case of the novel. With a combination of experience, imagination and technique, the attempt is made to pierce through the surface and to dig deeply into the selected segment. The exploration tries to cut through to the depths of life and confront realities often hidden from daily perception. Superficial inanities are not on the artistic agenda. The writer's vocation is the serious one of observing and illuminating through precise observation the deeper issues of human existence. It is surely at this level, too, that the Church would wish to live, and so ought to be grateful to the one who can open up a vision on lived human existence, in poem, novel or drama.

The media world

The need is most urgent today for an artistic spirit that will explore the depths at a time when elements of the media tend in the opposite direction. Advertisements in bold colours, breathless voices and loud music promise paradise; all is simple, no pain, no strain, no hardship. News reports are mainly soundbite driven. Never in human history were such quantities of news, facts and figures poured out upon people on a daily basis. Never before was information so immediate – missiles are fired on camera, war is waged in the living-room. The reporting regularly borders on the sensational and melodramatic, accompanied by rapidly altering images, electronic music and the constant screaming of the scandalous. Each thirty-minute news bulletin must have a new story, no pausing or time for reflection. Determined by the commercial necessity of keeping its audience, the world of the soundbite is for the simplification of all that is complex; trading only in black and white and ever aiming to entertain with the spectacular, the facile and the banal. The range of human emotions behind these headlines is not captured and there is the sense of living in a world of silhouettes. Cardinal Martini observes that: 'The drift towards mere entertainment is the easiest and most dangerous tendency that faces the media. It's a logic that insists on staying on the surface of everything.'[3] The trends in this direction are so strong that even some reflective journalists themselves are now becoming alarmed at the pressure to be drawn into the world of myth, rumour and inaccuracy, where truth can be distorted for the sake of the catchy headline. Their concern is that human beings will become incapable of attending to calm and considered reporting when the sensational and spectacular are at hand to provide sensory stimulation and excitement twenty-four hours per day.

Superficial audience
There is a lot of agreement that this spin towards superficiality in media is pushing humans in a similar direction. The ability to nuance is lessened and the shadings that a realistic judgement of life demands are not to be learned on the current affairs programme. Umberto Eco refers to the

---

3. Carlo Maria Martini, *Communicating Christ to the World*, Kansas City: Sheed and Ward, 1994, p. 95.

'distracted attitude to which mass communications have accustomed us'.[4] Again Cardinal Martini articulates the point with clarity: 'With the remote control in hand, we have the impression of being in control of the TV. But zapping ends up producing a fragmented use of the medium, an incessant search for pleasing images, creating what analysts call "TV flux", that is, a flood of disconnected images.'[5] Being pummelled by such an amalgam of sounds, images, colours and impulses, genuine human feeling can be numbed, sensibilities can be deadened and the distinction between fact and fiction can be destroyed. In the context the poet asks: 'I wonder if many people feel as I do – that in the society we have created it is very difficult to give your full, sustained attention to anything or anybody for long?'[6] In this media landscape the vocation of the serious writer is to be treasured more than ever. The world needs the voice that will pause and be still, enter the complexities of human stories and communicate these imaginatively. While a report may list the statistics for emigration, such abstraction can never convey the pain and uncertainty that Brian Friel portrays in *Philadelphia Here I Come*. Nor will the playwright's profound exploration of the tension between father and son be material for the news headlines. The artist is one of the saviours of a humanity that is under serious threat from hysterical reporting and superficial advertising. In this attempt to prevent life from being reduced to banalities by a media culture, the Church and artist are surely on the same platform.

---

4. Umberto Eco, 'Hope for the New Millennium', *Doctrine and Life*, January 1998, p. 6.
5. Ibid.
6. Brendan Kennelly, *The Book of Judas*, Newcastle upon Tyne: Bloodaxe Books, p. 11.

The challenge to accepted views

The depths of situations which the writer unearths may have remained concealed for many reasons. One possible reason is that a particular society may be unwilling to face certain dimensions of itself. The vision of the writer is therefore likely to disturb and challenge the popular view. History shows how the playwright's text has been censored and the actor's words have sparked a riot. The reason is understandable and a compliment to the writer. The artist can see deeper than the political slogan, the psychological jargon, the ecclesiastical rhetoric. When veneers are pushed aside, genuine questions are exposed and these may not be popularly accepted. One might recall how the poets of the First World War, like Owen, Sassoon, or Brooke, challenged the adage 'Dulce et decorum est pro patria mori'. That willingness to challenge and the courage to disturb could also be put on the Church agenda. This prophetic dimension of the artistic vocation, digging beneath the surface, can hardly be ignored by the theologian who shares in the same prophetic spirit, being called to search under the exterior to discern the hidden presence of God.

Digging for truth

Perhaps constant absorption in the mundane and even the superficial may so numb people that they become disturbed by the issues presented by the artist. They may never even have dreamed that such depths lay beneath the surface. The serious writer, attentive to the real issues in the lives of the characters created, will often shatter appearances in the painful effort to articulate the truth in all its rawness. Delving beneath the surface of apparent well-being, the writer unearths a hidden world and reveals that appearances are seldom what they seem. The reader might prefer to ignore many aspects of that world and instead find superficial appearances more comfortable. But with eyes newly opened we are challenged to face the revelation. Often behind smooth tranquillity lies turbulence and discord. The appearance of the gentle West of the John Hinde postcard, itself a work of photographic beauty, is shattered by the violent and bitter West of Martin McDonagh's *Leenane Trilogy*. Or how the perception of the happy Irish peasant in his fields was dramatically altered by the portrait of Paddy Maguire in Kavanagh's 'Great Hunger'. In criticism of institutionalised religion it has been said that it answers questions that are not being asked. Whether accurate or not, the comment points to the need for the Church and the theologian to be attentive to the voice that articulates the depth issues. It has been noted, for instance, that the characters in the recent plays of Bernard Farrell or Declan Hughes, or the novels of Dermot Bolger or Colum McCann are preoccupied with ecclesiastical issues. But the matters they deal with so painfully and so humorously, are earnest matter for theological reflection.

Looking into the face of darkness

Delving into truth is a noble, but often disturbing task. This becomes most apparent when the dark side of humanity has to be portrayed in all its starkness. In the visual arts the tranquillity of Constable's *Haywain* has given way to the work of Francis Bacon, whose endeavour was to depict the human cry with the whole coagulation of pain and despair. This darkness cannot be ignored. The point is made forcefully in a scene in the Thomas Mann story, 'Gladius Dei'. The character Hieronymus, furious at the dreadful quality of a picture of the Madonna on sale in the dealer's window, screams at the seller: 'Do you think to wash over with lurid colours the misery of the world?'[7] Later he spells out the point which applies to all artists: 'Art is the holy torch which turns its light upon all frightful depths, all the shameful and woeful abysses of life.'[8] The American Catholic writer, Flannery O'Connor, insisted on the importance of the writer attending to the reality of evil and the constant temptation to deny its existence and power. She was aware that when the depth of human existence is sounded, there one finds much to mourn. The writer confronts us with the little sins and larger evils that lurk within the human heart. Only the one who is aware that, given favourable conditions, he too could kill, should be cast in the role of Macbeth. The journalist Fergal Keane noted recently that the murderers of the world are not deranged monsters but human beings like ourselves placed in different situations. Theological reflection must listen to the voice of the creative writer when the dark side of human life is articulated, if for no other reason than to provide a deeper understanding of the depth of sinfulness from which humanity needs to be redeemed. 'To speak in the language of Christian theology it is precisely by acknowledging our status as fallen creatures, alienated from God, that we enter into a right and truthful relationship to God; it is precisely as sinners that God's grace meets us and justifies us.'[9]

The cry of suffering humanity

One aspect of that darkness is the pain and suffering of human beings that the writer places before us. We are faced

---

7. Thomas Mann, *Little Herr Friedmann and Other Stories*, London: Minerva, 1997, p. 120.
8. Ibid.
9. George Pattiston, *Art, Modernity and Faith*, London: Macmillan, 1991, p. 109.

repeatedly with 'the weariness, the fever and the fret here, where men sit and hear each other groan' (Keats, 'Ode to a Nightingale'). Recent Irish drama has provided a strong illustration of the writer's attention to this theme of pain, from the break-up of family and indeed community life in Friel's *Dancing at Lughnasa*, to the tragedy of war in MacGuinness' *Observe the Sons of Ulster Marching towards the Somme*, and the loneliness and pain of the outsider in many of the plays of Tom Murphy. The artist cannot avoid the world's pain, because when one looks deeply into life, one soon sees into suffering. The theologian Walter Kasper has observed that the widespread expulsion of suffering from public life 'by hiding it behind a mask of youthfulness, vitality and health leads to an alarming shallowness and impoverishment of our experience and a declining sensitivity.... No one has experienced humanity to the full unless he or she has experienced its finiteness and suffering'.[10] We depend so often on the creative writer to push aside the veneer and enable us to glimpse and be touched by the pain of our world, perhaps especially in places and people where we might not have expected it. A Church that hopes to be in touch with the pain of the world must therefore give ear to what the writer observes of the pain in the human heart.

The beauty of being human
The attention to the dark is of course balanced by a reflection on the positive, the good and the beautiful in human life. There is much to celebrate and the writer cannot fail to linger here. Seamus Heaney comments on the need to balance what is destructive with what is promising, on 'the need to have

---

10. Walter Kasper, *The God of Jesus Christ*, London: SCM Press, 1983, p. 84.

space in my reckoning and imagining for the marvellous as well as for the murderous'.[11] It is not, however, that the good and evil exist side by side in life just as in Shakespeare, who explores at one time the evil ambition of Macbeth and then on another occasion the gentle love of Romeo and Juliet. Rather, and more profoundly, the good and bad, and the yearnings in both directions, are intertwined and interwoven in an intricate complexity and the artist is constantly laying bare the closeness of the two and their mutual effects on each other. The writer shows how pain and happiness are profoundly close in every human situation, and every relationship is simultaneously coloured with shades of each. Yet the dark does not always prevail. Sebastian Barry's portrayal of the old RIC man, Thomas Dunne, in *The Steward of Christendom*, leaves no doubt about how human gentleness and dignity triumphs in spite of a life of fracture and the loneliness and cruelty of a Baltinglass institution.

The orator of the human condition

Presenting to the world the depth of its darkness and suffering, its joys and hopes, the writer is thus presenting the human condition. Here is humanity, capable of amazing greatness and deathly destruction; with yearnings towards happiness and finding only misery; with admirable qualities of bravery and despicable cowardice; divine-like love and diabolical hate. The picture of the human condition is thus one of amazing contradiction. Polarities towards good and evil abound and at times can hardly be distinguished. This emerges most forcefully when the writer explores human motivation, and illustrates the intertwining of love and hate,

11. Seamus Heaney, *Nobel Lecture*, December 1995.

possessiveness and detachment, generosity and meanness, within the same human relationship.

Speaking from the heart of that confrontation with the human condition, the artist would surely warn the Church, both to take gravely the darkness in the human heart, and to ensure also the need to balance this with attention to the light. Acknowledging the complexity of their relating, the artist may be saying that much of life will be lived in grey, where there is indeed light, but light always in danger of consumption by the surrounding darkness. To ignore either light or darkness, or to fail to appreciate their intricate interweaving, is to be in danger of superficial response to the human condition and dissipate energies in what may prove irrelevancies.

Windows of wonder, doors to mystery

When we encounter the human condition in the novel, play or poem, with all its contradictions and paradoxes, there is evoked the sense of wonder. In an age characterised by busyness and rushing, constantly changing images and information, there is little time to wonder, less opportunity to pause and be aware of the strangeness and the miracle that is the human situation. The old school rhyme asked 'What if this world is so full of care we have not time to stand and stare?' One of the most powerful gifts that art brings the world is to cause us to pause, and pay attention and open our eyes in wonder. In a story of many years ago, 'The Windows of Wonder', by the recently deceased Bryan McMahon, a young teacher discovers the incredible power of storytelling to bring life and laughter to a class of children deadened by a narrow educational system. In an enthusiastic statement of her conviction she told the children, 'Your eyes are like rooms that are dark or brown. But somewhere in the rooms, if only you will pull aside the heavy curtains, you will find windows – these are the windows of wonder'.[12] The poet Patrick Kavanagh represents all artists when he speaks of the endeavour to 'charm back the luxury of a child's soul' to see 'the newness that was in every stale thing'.[13]

The artist has the gift of opening a door into the dark and the chink of light evokes amazement. Our hearts and spirits sense some glimmer of the mystery that is life. 'All real poems, all great novels and plays, begin and end in the mystery of who we are and how we relate to each other and the world.'[14] This encounter with mystery can occur in all kinds of experiences of life but the artist must remain as one of the privileged purveyors of mystery. 'Art has an almost unparalleled power to express the human condition and to raise the question as to the meaning and coherence of existence as a whole.'[15] Here is a hint of the transcendent. This is not to suggest that art is a replacement for religion, but it is to take seriously the words of Wendy Beckett: 'It is not a substitute for religion, but for those who have no other access to God it is a valid means of entering into the numinous dimension that alone makes the 'incomprehensibility' not only bearable but life-giving.'[16] Within theology, the importance of religious experience has again received attention in recent decades. Without awe and wonder in the

---

12. Michael Mayne, *This Sunrise of Wonder*, London: Fount, 1995, p. 181.
13. 'Advent'.
14. George Pattiston, *Art, Modernity and Faith*, London: Macmillan, 1991, p. 110.
15. Ibid.
16. Wendy Beckett, *Art and the Sacred*, p. 9.

face of the Incomprehensible there can be no religious worship. Only with gratefulness for the sacramentality of all life can one value the sacramental celebrations of the Church. Consequently, the notion of mystery has returned to the heart of theology. Nowhere is this more excitingly obvious than in reflection on the Trinity. What once seemed a sterile exercise to solve an elaborate conundrum, is now an exciting engagement with Ultimate Mystery, against which all other mysteries, especially humanity, are pale reminders and indicators. The writer immersed in the mystery of the human and the myriad wonders contained within it, offers us the possibility of having our spirits made more sensitive to the Mysterium Tremendum, whom the Church names God. In the poem, play, short story and novel we may indeed dip 'our fingers in the pockets of God'.[17] Art is not a conclusion, but a stepping-stone towards deeper awareness.

17. Patrick Kavanagh, 'The Long Garden'.

MEDITATION ON A PAINTING

Pat O'Brien

In front of me as I write this is a reproduction of a painting from the National Gallery in Dublin. It is *Kitchen Maid with the Supper at Emmaus* by Velázquez. I cannot remember my first encounter with this early work by the Spanish artist but over the years it has accumulated more and more meaning for me, has become like a sacred place. I pilgrim to it as often as possible. Each visit reveals another aspect, as indeed the history of the painting itself includes moments of new discovery. Only during a gallery cleaning in 1933 did the figures of Jesus and his two companions sitting at table emerge from under the pentimenti of the centuries. And, like everything in life, the full story of the painting will never be known, the complete picture. At some stage of its history the canvas was cut and all we have of one of the disciples is a hand gesturing in the air. Because we cannot see his face or the contours of his body, the meaning of the gesture is uncertain. Is it an expression of disillusion, the disappointment of the death of Jesus still gnawing at his heart ('We had thought that he would be the one to set Israel free' – perhaps the most poignant and revealing line in scripture)? Or is it the arm flung out in sudden joy at the realisation that the stranger they met along the road is revealed as the Risen Christ? Whatever. The hand in many ways has become the hand of the viewer before the questions and the glory of this painting. I would like to meditate on some of the levels of this work in terms of my life and the reasons I remain in the Church and find sustenance from both the gospel and the work of artists and writers.

Kitchen Maid with the Supper at Emmaus is a *bodegón* painting, a mixture of stilllife and kitchen or tavern setting. Indeed, this one must also include the vital element of a portrait painting because the 'Kitchen Maid' herself is a masterly study of exhaustion and hope. Her face is the profile of an oppression that names itself and begins the journey to freedom. A new light illumines one side of her face, the other half remains occluded. There is attentiveness in the face, which suggests that she is something beyond the bare necessities of the table that supports her. The poet Denise Levertov captures this perfectly in a work inspired by this painting:

> She listens, listens, holding
> her breath. Surely that voice
> is his – the one
> who had looked at her, across the crowd,
> as no one had ever looked?
> Had seen her? Had spoken as if to her?

Surely those hands were his,
taking the platter of bread from hers just now?
hands he'd laid on the dying and made them well?

Surely that face –?

The man they'd crucified for sedition and blasphemy.
The man whose body disappeared from its tomb.
The man it was rumoured now some women had seen
    this morning, alive?

Those who had brought this stranger home to their
    table
don't recognise yet with whom they sit.
But she is in the kitchen, absently touching
the winejug she's to take in,
a young Black servant intently listening,

swings round and sees
the light around him
and is sure.

Without the 1933 recovery of the gospel scene, the bearing of the woman contains it anyway. And this strikes me as important for our consideration of religion and the arts in today's world. The event of the Resurrection has changed history forever. Even if the figure of the Risen Christ is unrecognised, or ignored, or disappears under the avalanche of today's media and noise, or is deliberately airbrushed from history like figures around portraits of Stalin, he waits in the shadows. Great works of art and literature emerge from a world where the Risen One has walked, still bearing the scars and scabs of his crucifixion. There was a time when this linking of culture to Christ would not seem strange or even contradictory. The Renaissance saw the Church and the artistic community as one. The great painters were sponsored by the Church and their great galleries were the cathedrals and monasteries of Europe. The poet whose influence is still felt in Irish literature today (in the work of Seamus Heaney and Thomas Kinsella in particular), Dante Alighieri, explored his age through the otherwords of the Christian mysteries. The procession of his feet is sacred. But the common perception today is that this ancient alliance is broken, that the worlds of the Church and the artist are contradictory. In Ireland this perception is highlighted more than in other places by our history of censorship and distrust. Joyce's 'Non serviam' is seen as a declaration of treason by the writers against the state of the Church. So much of the daily commentary in the media is funded by such a disregard for the Church that the prevailing attitude is that the Church has nothing to offer society, that it has no insights to explore our time and that its time is over. Some sort of secular future, a post-Christian society, is held to be the ideal, and the artefacts of that civilisation will be music, poetry, films and art that will have no sense of the sacred, the transcendent.

This is an attitude that needs to be addressed at a very serious level. Not just in defence of the Church, and its vision of our humanity, its long meditation and mediation of the divine presence in the world, but also in the name of the deep reach and echo of the artistic quest. An art that doesn't wonder before the unknown, that refuses the silences at the edge of the human scale, that will not hear the prayer in the breathing of the earth, is doomed to the ephemeral and the passing. It will no longer challenge, open the windows of wonder, face us with the dark questions with which history confronts us. There is hardly a modern writer of worth who is not involved in the exploration of the Resurrection. Daniel Murphy's book *Christianity and Modern European Literature* is a lucid and invigorating discussion of the work of twelve major writers who are explicitly Christian in theme and sensibility. His analysis covers the range and diversity of the faith. His subjects – Dostoevsky, Tolstoy, Unamuno, Mauriac, Eliot, Pasternak, Mandelstam, Akhmatova, Auden, White, Milosz and Brodsky – represent many strands of Christianity, but are united in commitment to the world that saves. It would be easy to add other important writers to Murphy's contents. One thinks of Böll and our own Francis Stuart, in different ways confronting love in the dark night of Nazi Germany; the Japanese novelist Shusaku Endo examining the Christian story in an alien landscape; or Flannery O'Connor in the furious environs of the Southern States seeking Wisdom; the plays of Beckett which are set in the silence of Golgotha, the bare minimal words of comfort. Around the ancient pilgrim island of Lough Derg three of our own major poets have set important works of self-examination. Patrick Kavanagh, Denis Devlin and Seamus Heaney are all in search there for that transcendent note that is heard wherever the religious or artistic mind is set loose.

The list of writers is long, yet limited. And yet in many highly regarded works of literary criticism this vital element of their work is ignored. As if the secondary sources of culture, the critics and review writers, are unable or unwilling to deal with this religious impulse. The fires of Pentecost, the new language of the Church, is too hot to handle. This is a woeful disregard for the genius of these people, and is a deep loss to many who might be brought into contact with their work in their own search for understanding of their faith in difficult times. In the work of most of the people I have mentioned the centrality of Christianity is explicit. They make no dead bones about it. In one of his first comments on the novel he was then beginning, *Doctor Zhivago*, Boris Pasternak wrote to his cousin: 'The mood of this piece is set by my Christianity... deriving from various aspects of the Gospels in addition to the ethical aspect.' Milosz insists in his diary of reflections, *A Year of the Hunter,* that all his poetry 'continues to preserve the remnants of a relation to objective truth, to God'. Many other artists and writers are less overt, but any work that is created out of the deepest and truest impulse is its own testimony to hidden light. In some the figures in the painting are seen, in others they are covered over, but the glance of their characters is towards the stranger in the other room.

The setting of this painting in a tavern is important to me for several reasons. It seems to me that one of the reasons the Church today has lost its credibility in Ireland is that it no longer has a sense of the sacredness of everything, that idea which is at the root of our beginnings. Celtic Christianity had a vision of everything redeemed. In the poetry and art of that period there is a blessedness on all creation. The Trinity of God is imprinted not just on the shamrock but in the rocks, the sea, the sky, the work of human hands, the hovering of windhover and angels. Since then we have made divisions between the sacred and the profane. With the result that the mystery of the Eucharist has verged into the magical. This painting reminds me always that there are three Eucharists in the life of Jesus. One before the Crucifixion and the Resurrection, the one usually referred to as the Last Supper. Although it is obviously part of a ritual ceremony it has the freedom of a meal, epitomised by the secret dramas that are at work around the table. We have turned it into a formal Church gathering, surrounded by rules and piety. The Eucharists of the Risen Christ have the exuberance and anarchy of the Spirit at work. The roadside tavern on the way to Emmaus and the meal shared with his friends on the lakeshore after a night's fishing speak of a new world where all is drenched with the divine. In laying stress on the specialness of the sacraments we lose our ancient sense of the sacrament that is the world. And it is only in this broader context that the sacraments have any meaning. To receive communion in church is to create communion in the world, to help the people of the world recover their common humanity before the table of the earth. There is an implied ethics which at one bite of the bread, one sup of the wine, undermines any justification of war, violence, oppression. The breaking of the bread is the breaking of a new sun over a new world. Christ at the tavern will shortly disappear from sight, leaving the two disciples to run back with news of the Risen One and the Kitchen Maid to preside over the table. She is the servant, the slave, the black, the oppressed whose freedom is declared.

The foreground of the painting comprises the still-life element of the *bodegón*. There are jugs and dishes, a water jar, an upturned cup, a mortar and pestle. A bulb of garlic lies on the right-hand side of the table. And although their spacing is masterly and leaves room for the human figure to dominate the centre there is no sense of deliberate artistic licence in the formation. One feels that the woman placed them like this after the task of rinsing and drying. There is nothing exotic in the display. No rainbow of flowers, no orchard of fruits. The beauty is in the everyday. Except for the bulb of garlic they are all 'the work of human hands'. The table is carpeted, the utensils have all known the hands of the potter. Velázquez gives to each item the weight of its creation. Such is the power of his hand that one can almost feel the glisten from just-washed delft. Every time I look at this painting I think of a Buddhist saying which brings us to the heart of things: 'After the ecstasy, wash the dishes'. The religious task is to find in the everyday the meaning of life. One of the great wonders of Christianity is its insistence on the incarnation, that the Son of God became human, that he shared in the daily toil. A religion that constantly seeks the miraculous, the defeat of nature, cannot help us come to terms with our humanity. As public life in this country exiles the religious to the margins there is a great danger that many are attracted to the exotic and the otherworldly, to seek God as an escape from the quotidian. Still lifes like this return us to the ordinary, to the tasks of home and factory, of school and church, to find the Risen One in the rising bread in the oven, in the gardener who plants spring flowers. There is something else on the table, which, although as ordinary as a piece of cloth, haunts with suggestion. It is directly in front of the woman, in the centre of the table, with free space around it. Look at it long enough and it becomes the very focus point of the whole painting. What is it? Beyond doubt it is a piece of material used to dry the utensils. It is rolled up, squashed after use. It might be linen. Why does it haunt? The artist must have a reason for placing it so precisely here. It demands an answer. Remember, we are talking about a painting of the Risen Christ. Once we realise this a gospel passage from St John echoes unerringly in the mind, 'Simon Peter who was following now came up, went right into the tomb, saw the linen cloths on the ground, and also the cloth that had been over his head; this was not with the linen cloths but rolled up in a place by itself.' At once we see the common utensils, the work of potter and servant girl, as signs and reality of the Risen One. They and she alive in the room of the once dead. The ordinary is bathed in the light of the Resurrection. This insight is deepened when we see where the main gathering place of the light is in this painting. It is on the white skull-cap worn by the Kitchen Maid. A section is missing near the top. We are in intoxicating depths of perception.

There is an even more revolutionary moment on the edge of declaring itself in this painting. In the distant room Jesus Christ is about to bless the bread, his right hand is raised in the gesture. In a moment he will break the bread and be recognised by the two disciples. At that same moment the Kitchen Maid is about to raise the jug of wine from her table. Velázquez is painting a remarkable tableau of the shared priesthood of all in Jesus Christ. And, perhaps much more than just this, the moment of consecration in our Eucharist in this painting is shared by Jesus Christ and the Kitchen Maid. He lifts the bread, she the wine. This painting should become the emblem of the movement for the ordination of women.

The Kitchen Maid is obviously a Moor, and in giving her a central role in this painting in seventeenth-century Spain Velázquez is clearly making a statement about human equality and shared dignity. Inevitably when viewing this I think of the oppressed people of other places. Given the Spanish background I think of El Salvador, of Archbishop Romero martyred while saying Mass, of the six Jesuit priests massacred on the lawn of their home. And, in light of this painting, I think of their housekeeper and her daughter killed with them. The beauty of the gospel is measured in the cost paid by so many. It is counted out also in the work of artists and writers who dare to explore the consequences for human life won by the life, death and resurrection of Jesus Christ, Beyond both Church and culture is that conquest of death that both serve. Or sadly sometimes do not serve. The Church has too often been the slave to forces of death, has too often imprisoned people in fear, or submitted its people to armies of destruction. The history of culture is equally bloody. For every Pasternak, Mandelstam, Akhmatova or Camus there were hundreds who wrote hymns of praise to Stalin, or painted posters to Socialist Realism while the brave artists suffered the destruction of their work. The struggle to stay true to life itself, in all its riches and depths, is never easy. There are temptations for everyone to betray our first trust.

But when gospel and human expression are at their best, their most daring and original, we take hope. In the lives of some Christians the Word of God takes on the perfection of a Velázquez or a Van Gogh or a Picasso. And there are writers and artists and musicians whose lives and works have the halo of sanctity. In a magnificent passage in *Doctor Zhivago* Pasternak expresses this double helix which is the basis of all life. Zhivago's uncle is speaking: 'What you don't understand is that it is possible to be an atheist, it is possible not to know if God exists or why he should, and yet to believe that man does not live in a state of nature but in history, and that history as we know it now began with Christ. It is founded on the Gospels. Now what is history? Its beginning is that of the centuries of systematic work devoted to the solution of the enigma of death, so that death itself may eventually be overcome. That is why people write symphonies, and why they discover mathematical infinity and electromagnetic waves....' Or why a painter named Velázquez once painted *Kitchen Maid with the Supper at Emmaus*. In it the Gospel story is imagined again in paint. It is explored for contemporary meaning. The act of painting itself speaks of the creativity at the heart of existence. And both the Risen Christ and this painting have resonance today which deserve our attention. Here and in Church the cloth of death is rolled up and the canvas of life reaches out its hand to embrace us.

THE CHURCH AND THE ARTIST

Mark Patrick Hederman OSB

Artists have had a pre-eminent place in the Church since its foundation. Artists wrote the Gospels, artists created the specific form of Christian art in the icons, artists built and decorated the cathedrals of Christendom. Yeats regarded Byzantium as the place and the time when art and religion combined most felicitously and produced the highest and furthest reaches of the human spirit. If he could have been given the privilege of spending some time in any place at any moment of history, he would have chosen Byzantium, where Christian art received its most unique stamp.

I shall confine my remarks to another less exciting or exemplary period in the collaboration between the Church and art, namely the relationship between the Catholic Church in Ireland and artists during this century, and my paper will be divided into two parts. The first will describe the relationship as it has been; the second will suggest what that relationship might be in the future.

I can only describe that relationship over the last eighty or so years as pretty dreadful and convey its texture in a story. It is not even my story. There are two women who come to pray before a life-sized crucifix in a church in Dublin. I presume they are women because men so rarely pray before crucifixes. They do not get on well with each other. The first is kneeling in front of the crucifix and sees the other approaching behind her, waiting for her to finish so that she can take her place at the foot of the cross. Devotee number one therefore decides to extend her prayer and redouble her devotion to keep her rival out of the goalmouth. Devotee number two waits patiently behind her and eventually realises that the opposition is prolonging this visitation for the express purpose of keeping her away from Our Lord. So she leans over the kneeling figure and whispers to the crucified: 'O Lord Jesus, wouldn't you take the nail out of your foot and drive it into her eye.'

White, male, heterosexual, Roman Catholic nationalists may have been supportive of the ideals and comfortable with the reality that became the Ireland of the third, fourth and fifth decades of this century. Far from the kind of dialogue between the Catholic Church and the arts that would have been both salutary and invigorating, there developed an atmosphere of fear and suspicion which was expressed and enshrined in the Censorship Act passed in 1929. The answer to creative interrogation and criticism on the part of artists was to silence them. In the sixty years between 1929 and 1989 when the act became, for all practical purposes, dormant, almost every important Irish writer, from Liam O'Flaherty in 1930 to Lee Dunne in 1976, had books banned in Ireland, as indeed, had Proust, Faulkner, Hemingway, Saul Bellow, Nabokov, Emile Zola, Sartre and Nadine Gordimer, to mention just a few. Many artists protested vigorously against this act, perhaps none more eloquently than George Bernard Shaw:

> In the nineteenth century all the world was concerned about Ireland. In the twentieth, nobody outside Ireland cares twopence what happens to her…. If, having broken England's grip of her, she slops back into the Atlantic as a little grass patch in which a few million moral cowards

are not allowed to call their souls their own by a handful of morbid Catholics, mad with heresyphobia, unnaturally combining with a handful of Calvinists mad with sexphobia ... then the world will let 'these Irish' go their way into insignificance without the smallest concern.[1]

This situation developed mainly because the Church was identified with the hierarchy and the moral majority and not acknowledged as the community founded by Jesus Christ and anointed by the Holy Spirit as the covenant of God's will to unite the whole human family within the fullness of the life of the Trinity, so that their salvation might reach to the ends of the earth.

The Church as it was intended was built on the foundations of the apostles and the prophets. We are inclined to understand these two foundations as one thing and to say this sentence as if it were two ways of saying the same thing; almost as we say 'post and telegraphs' or 'bacon and eggs'. But these are not the same thing; each of these foundations represents a fundamentally distinct principle. In the context of our present discussion, the archbishop is one and the artist is the other.

We are talking about tradition, about the handing on of the truth, the very basis of our belief in Christianity. This word 'tradition', as has often been pointed out, is the same word in Latin (*tradere*) for handing on, or handing over. It can also be used – and is used in the Gospels – for the handing over of Jesus to the soldiers by Judas, in other words, for 'betrayal'.

---

1. 'The Censorship', *Irish Statesman II* (1928), reprinted in *Banned in Ireland: Censorship and the Irish Writer*, edited by Julia Carlson, University of Georgia Press, Athens, 1990, pp. 133-138.

There have been moments in the history of the Church when the truth was maintained by only one or two people – one or two prophets; all the rest had fled or had betrayed it. Such a moment is recorded in the life of Maximus the Confessor, who alone bore witness to the fundamental truth for all of us, including the three persons of the Trinity, that there were two wills in the person of Jesus Christ, a human will and a divine will. Everyone else in the official Church, including the Pope of the time, was supporting what later became known as the monothelite heresy, which declared anathema anyone who held that there was more than one will in the person of Jesus Christ. Maximus was martyred by officialdom, had his limbs cut off and his tongue cut out, but he stubbornly maintained what he knew to be true. His protest, his courage, his self-imposed exile from the official Church of his day, not only forced that same Church to acknowledge his personal sanctity, but it also ensured that all future officialdom would be obliged to support and uphold the point of view which he so stubbornly and singlehandedly refused to abandon.

The message of the artists to us, since the beginning of this century, has been pretty consistent and has been stubbornly repudiated or ignored by officialdom in the Church. And the message is this: the picture of humanity that you are painting, whether in its ideal form or in your perception of what it is actually like, is too narrow, too pessimistic, too 'other-worldly', too unsubtle. You refuse to accept the blood-and-guts reality of what we are, the bodily, sexual, earthy amalgam that makes us who we are. The French philosopher Lachelier is supposed to have woken up one morning at the age of twenty-six, saying to himself: 'This morning I realise that I am the son of a man and a woman; that disappoints me: I thought I was a little more than that.'

We don't want to be more than that. We want to be human, fully human. We believe that God so loved our humanity that he sent his only son to share it with us and to make it part of his life. You are trying to deny that reality, trying to create your own picture of what that humanity should be like if it is to be worthy of such relationship. We say, No. If God doesn't want our humanity the way it is, the way he made it, then he doesn't want us at all. He wants something else. The job of the artist is to describe, to express that reality as it actually is. Artists have been doing that from the beginning of this century and especially in Ireland, and because they have been doing precisely that they have been condemned, banned, excommunicated by the official organs of the Church.

James Joyce was a religious man. He wasn't an atheist. He believed that the humanity being presented, endorsed, canonised by the Church was a fake. He gave his life and his work to defending the orthodoxy of humanity. In a letter to his brother Stanislaus in 1906 Joyce says: 'If I put a bucket into my own soul's well, sexual department, I draw up Griffith's and Ibsen's and Skeffington's and Bernard Vaughan's and St Aloysius' and Shelley's and Renan's water along with my own. And I am going to do that in my novel *(inter alia)* and plonk the bucket down before the shades and substances above mentioned to see how they like it: and if they don't like it I can't help them. I am nauseated by their lying drivel about pure men and pure women and spiritual love for ever: blatant lying in the face of the truth.'[2]

Unlike Milton, whose self-professed purpose was to describe the ways of God to humankind, Joyce wanted to describe as accurately as he knew how the ways of humankind

---

2. *Selected Joyce Letters,* edited by Richard Ellman, New York, 1975, p. 129.

to God. The Bible, which is also a work of artists, has been described by one rabbi as not so much a theology for humankind as an anthropology for God.

Rilke, Joyce's contemporary, made a similar protest:

> Why, I ask you, when people want to help us, who are often helpless, why do they leave us in the lurch just there at the root of all experience? Anyone who would stand by us there could rest satisfied that we should ask nothing further from him. For the help which he imparted to us there would grow of itself with our life, becoming, together with it, greater and stronger. And would never fail. Why are we not set in the midst of what is most mysteriously ours? How we have to creep round about it and get into it in the end; like burglars and thieves, we get into our own beautiful sex, in which we lose our way and knock ourselves and stumble and finally rush out of it again, like men caught transgressing.... Why, if guilt or sin had to be invented because of the inner tension of the spirit, why did they not attach it to some other part of the body, why did they let it fall on that part, waiting until it dissolved in our pure source and poisoned and muddied it? Why have they made our sex homeless, instead of making it the place for the festival of our competency? Why do we not belong to God from this point? My sex is not directed only towards posterity, it is the secret of my own life – and it is only because it may not occupy the central place there, that so many people have thrust it to the edge, and thereby lost their balance.[3]

---

3. Rainer Maria Rilke, 'The Young Workman's Letter' (written in February 1922), from *Rodin and Other Prose Pieces,* London 1986, pp. 151-152.

Throughout this century in Ireland we have been told the same thing in different ways, by Edna O'Brien and John McGahern, for instance. None of these is saying that there is no God, there is no Church, there is no Christianity. On the contrary, they are suggesting that if any of these realities want to have some effective contact with us and operate any kind of comprehensive salvation, they must begin taking seriously the partner with whom they are trying to have such a relationship.

When Sinead O'Connor publicly tears up a picture, it is not because she is an atheist or because she doesn't believe in the Church. It is an act of frustration and disappointment at a particular presentation of the Church and its failure to speak to the kind of people we really are, the people we have painstakingly become and are not prepared to renounce or to betray. In a recent interview she says: 'I've always been a religious person... I consider myself to be a Christian person.... I also believe that out of all this there'll probably end up being a very good Church... a good healthy Church that's doing its job.... If you deny sexuality then you deny God.... So how can you expect priests not to be sexually abusive if they have to deny their sexuality or believe that there's something wrong with it?... So once they let women in – which I'm sure they will eventually – I reckon they'll have a really united Church that'll be an inspiration to the rest of the world.'[4]

When I read Roddy Doyle I cry with laughter, not just because it is so funny but because it is so true. This is accurate cardiography of the present-day heartbeat. And it is too bad if the magisterium of the Catholic Church is

4. 'The Gospel according to Sinead', Interview with Olaf Tyaransen, Hot Press, 28 May 1997, p. 21.

disapproving, is saying no: you've got to change all that, you've got to go back to what we were like in the 1940s. We are not going back. And, anyway, the 1940s were nothing like you are pretending they were. Read *Angela's Ashes*.[5] They were terrible times for most people, and those who were pretending to be upright and virtuous according to your standards have all too recently been shown, for the most part, to be hypocritical and pathetically incapable of self-control. Your so-called virtue was for the most part simply impotence or incapacity to accede to any kind of virtue whatsoever.

Such, as I understand it, would be the case made by artists in this century against the Church. It is derived, also in my view, from the Church's view of human nature, of natural law and of the prescriptive and omniscient role and mandate of the Church's magisterium not just in matters of faith but also in the realms of morality and socio-political activity. It seems to me that a different kind of guidance and guardianship should dictate its role in the last two areas to that which determines its mandate in the first.

In a book called *Hidden Histories of Science,* five of the most gifted scientific writers in the world tell us in a series of different essays how science is influenced by culture and how misleading images and entrenched prejudices have distorted our view of life. The notion of evolution, for instance, or development, even etymologically, is mistakenly assumed to be the revelation of an already immanent structure or the unfolding of an already encoded and implicit pre-existing history.

These scientists suggest that such a model is inadequate and fails to do justice to the complexity of survival strategies and the creative ingenuity required of us to initiate and

---

5. Frank McCourt's autobiography, *Angela's Ashes*, London: HarperCollins, 1996.

maintain the kind of life that establishes the delicate balance between sovereignty and surrender.

It is not enough to obey laws that are already laid down; we have to create patterns and structures that are life-enhancing and that never existed before.

'Every species is the process of creating and re-creating, both beneficially and detrimentally, its own conditions of existence, its own environment.'[6] Some neurologists even suggest that far from being genetically determined or assigned to fixed nuclei or modules in the brain,[7] our higher cortex, where our higher learning occurs, is a malleable surface, 'uncommitted at birth', whose development 'depends on the particularities of life experience'. In other words, these scientists are sympathetic to the notion that nature, far from being a static, pre-existing, unchangeable programme, is, at the higher levels of its development, 'an emerging, self-creating whole,[8] which not only adapts to its environment but emerges under the influence of experience'.

This would mean that there is no possibility of someone in the sixth century BC, or the first or the thirteenth century CE, legislating for appropriate human behaviour in absolute terms. We are changing, we are the creative architects of our own evolution. This does not mean that we embrace the pragmatic and entirely opportunistic strategy of a situation ethics. It does mean that we reject the eternal, ever-present pre-determined and pre-determining structure, substance and texture of a so-called law which would imply that we who live in the twentieth

---

6. R.C. Lewontin, 'Genes, Environment and Organisms', *Hidden Histories of Science*, ed. Robert Silvers, London, 1997, p. 136.
7. Oliver Sacks, 'Scotoma: Forgetting and Neglect in Science', in Robert Silvers, op. cit., p. 177.
8. Ibid, p.179.

century and are about to enter the twenty-first are irrevocably and irredeemably the same as those members of our species who have inhabited the planet since time began.

We are different because we have made ourselves different. This difference has been a combination of environment and the human organism in a cooperative mutation. Those who have been most effective and inspirational in both detecting the changes necessary and imaging the adaptations to be accomplished have been artists and geniuses of one kind or another.

If we are to move forward towards a development which respects all the elements in the amalgam that we are, that we have become, that we hope to direct towards the most optimistic future, it is essential that the Church, which is the safeguard and the guarantor of God's presence among us, collaborates with the scientists and the artists who are the antennae, the diviners, the creators of our future: our eyes, our ears, our imaginations, our higher intellects, so that 'all shall be well and all manner of thing shall be well'.

In a recent interview Seamus Heaney made the following observation:

> My language and my sensibility is yearning to admit a kind of religious or transcendental dimension. But then there's the reality... the complacency and the utter simplification of these things into social instructions. That's what's disappointing.[9]

Artists are there also to shake our complacency and to refuse

---

9. Seamus Heaney, interviewed by Ian Hargreaves in *The Financial Times,* Monday, 10 June 1991.

'the utter simplification of "these things" into social instructions', Like Cézanne at the beginning of the century, Heaney has been trying to show us how to see, how to 'credit marvels' and balance the spirit level. His poetry and his criticism should become an essential part of the probing that determines the direction we now want to take. Artists are like scouts in the evolutionary march. Their work is to explore the territory ahead and advise on the paths to be tested.

Nor is it enough to say 'artists' and 'scientists' without reservation or discrimination. There is an ethic for the artist also, without obedience to which they become sterile or mediocre, greedy or irresponsible. There are good and bad artists just as there are good and bad bishops, good and bad scientists.

It seems to me that this was the subject of Brian Friel's last play, *Give Me your Answer Do*. Friel, let us remember, began his life on the road to priesthood. He left Maynooth after two years in the national seminary in the 1940s, where he explored the vocation which he believed he had for the priesthood.[10] In 1972, when he was forty-three years of age, he said: 'I hope that between now and my death I will have acquired a religion, a philosophy, a sense of life, that will make the end less frightening than it appears to me at this moment.'[11] The job of articulating just such a philosophy is partly the artist's, and Friel muses aloud about the possibility that our artists at this important time may have sold their integrity to the highest bidder instead of 'fashioning a conscience for their race'. Because, above all, what it seems to

---

10. Richard Pine, *Brian Friel and Ireland's Drama,* London, 1990, p. 17.
11. Quoted in Richard Pine, op.cit. p. 18.

me the artists are saying to the Church is this: There are truths which are absolute, there are dogmas which have to be preserved and written in stone in credal formulae and liturgical rites, but these are about the interventions of God among us. The truth about human beings, especially in relationship, is not such a truth. It cannot be captured in a formula. Art is the only medium subtle enough to express it.

And at this level, at this moment of difficulty and discovery, the role of the hierarchy in the Church might well be to discern rather than to dictate, to peruse rather than prescribe, to exercise their authority and responsibility in a more passive way, by examining the evidence produced and expressed by the scouts and the spies, before endorsing the strategy and confirming the direction that will lead us into the twenty-first century.

POETRY AND RELIGION

Mary O'Malley

'I don't love life as such; for me it begins to signify, that is to acquire weight and meaning, only when it is transformed, that is – in art. If I were to be taken beyond the ocean, into Paradise, and forbidden to write, I would refuse the ocean and paradise.' So wrote the great Russian poet Marina Tsvetaeva in her essay 'Art in the Light of Conscience'.

The late Octavio Paz has this to say in his essay 'Alternating Current': 'The difficulty of modern poetry does not stem from its complexity – Rimbaud is far simpler than Gongora or Donne – but rather from the fact that, like mysticism or love, it demands total surrender (and an equally total vigilance). If the word were not ambiguous, I would say that the nature of the difficulty is not intellectual, but *moral.*' Paz's reluctance to use the word moral is the reluctance of the poet to an amorphous word, to a word so general as to be rendered meaningless. Words such as soul, creativity and inspiration present us with the same dilemma. They are dangerous abstracts, vague, general and too often debased.

Such concepts need to be nailed to the particular. It is part of the poet's trade to be able to distinguish the quotidian from the mundane. Yet we believe in the given, or found poem. From where?

I believe all art is an act of faith as much as despair. What is poetry but 'words in search of the Word'? – as Paz says later in the same essay. And poets and artists use the symbols of their religion, whatever religion that may be, because they are powerful cyphers, and reasonably universal in what they convey. A good symbol is worth a book of abstraction. All the major religions used symbols to convey abstract ideas, or realities, as they used allegory. A poet, on a certain level, does the same thing. Yet Yeats, embracing the dangerous abstract with gusto, wrote of the soul as '...self-delighting, self-appeasing, self-affrighting', and we all know what he meant.

Although the priest and the poet might disagree profoundly as to its form, shape and relevance, they would be discussing the same territory. Many poets believe even more fervently in miracles than priests or shamans. Their language is often prayerful. They understand the nature of devotion and faith. But they have no certainty. Poetry cannot allow platitudes and half truths. The poet works in the service of truth and must go where that path leads. There are times of spiritual anguish to be endured, unfashionable as it is to speak of that nowadays. The dark night of the soul. Poets work in the light of the hell of human viciousness, and know the transforming power of human love. Where is God in all this? Perhaps it is on doubt that the artist becomes expert.

The relationship between art and religion, all religions, is often vexed and close. Whether we are talking about religion in its vibrant state, where faith flourishes, or the dead institution where the desperate place their last hopes, and are failed, there is still a connection. Poetry, in particular, knows the value of gods and their limitations, and religion the value of metaphor.

So where is the defining line? You could say it is a question of territory, that poems come from the same place as the mystic's vision. Or, the Czech poet Miroslav Holub would remind us, the schizophrenic's dreams. Be that as it may, art for the artist has the force and intensity of religion for the devout, possibly even the fanatic.

But there is another sense in which religion directly inspires or involves the poet. The Christian Church provided sensual delight and definite structure, as well as concepts of innocence and its opposite, defined by Blake as experience, and poets from Chaucer through the Metaphysical poets have drawn on those up to the present day. The same Blake said that every true poet, wittingly or unwittingly, is on the devil's side. So poets are every bit as contradictory as scripture.

As for myself, I want the old God back. I want him to be stern and good and keep everyone in line. I want to know that when people who are cruel and even downright evil die, he'll get them. I'd like a special little hot corner for people who sell weapons, and a room next door for the corporation members and county councillors who refuse to build public housing. And so on. I'd pray to that God every night, watch four (admittedly rather dark and quattrocento) angels perch at each corner of my bed, and sleep far more soundly than I do now. I don't object to the gender difference, nor the white beard, as long as I don't have to make him up, and I have no great objection to the devil, and he can keep the forked tail and the cloven hooves and the ability to come down at night as a great black cat, as long as he'll disappear with sparks flying out of him when I shower him with holy water.

I'd bow my head at the sound of a high communion bell and hear the Latin words that bring the living Christ into the Church. I want to be seven years of age, on the brink of reason, and I must live out my life knowing that I will never feel that radiant again. The loss of that childhood faith took years, but it was, and remains, the single most devastating experience of my life. It taught me the real meaning of the terms 'grace' and 'Fall'. Reason is not all it's cracked up to be. Religion will shrivel before base logic. So will art. Logic does not allow for the miraculous. Art does. I now see the consecration as a metamorphosis, but I used to believe it was a miracle. Poetry, the reading and the writing of it, has a certain complex and not entirely obvious link with the search for that lost radiance. But it is not a substitute religion. It is other, and the two cannot be confused. The symbolism of the religion I was brought up in has given me a store of metaphor, wooden crosses to nail down abstract nouns. It was, at the very least, well-defined. Full of muscular lines.

Each writer adds to that store as they grow and learn. My heaven has been replaced by a world, less male-centred essentially, with less certain gods, but also with slightly less room. I write to make sense of my world and, perhaps, occasionally, to transcribe or construct a message, a glimpse of another dimension through a rent in the everyday. There is no guarantee. Unlike religion, poetry makes few promises.

CONTRIBUTORS

Dermot Bolger is a poet, playwright and novelist, whose most recent novel, *Father's Music,* was written while a guest in All Hallows College.

Thomas Casey SJ works in the Jesuit university residence in Dublin.

Eamonn Conway is associate director of the Western Theological Institute, Galway.

Anthony Draper is a priest and lectures in theology at All Hallows College, Dublin.

Mark Patrick Hederman OSB is a monk in Glenstal Abbey.

Colum Kenny is a barrister, journalist and lecturer in communications.

Aidan Mathews is a writer who works with RTÉ radio. He has written several books, most recently *Lipstick on the Host* (fiction) and *According to the Small Hours* (poetry).

John Moriarty taught Literature and History of European Ideas at the University of Manitoba in Canada for seven years before returning to Ireland to work as a gardener.

Bernadette McCarrick works as a teacher, spiritual director and writer.

Breda O'Brien is a teacher and mother and a journalist with the *Sunday Business Post*.

Pat O'Brien is a priest of the diocese of Tuam and writes poetry.

Mary O'Malley is a poet whose most recent works are *The Knife in the Wave* and *Where the Rocks Float*.